Living on the

Borders

Living on the Borders

WHAT THE CHURCH CAN LEARN FROM ETHNIC IMMIGRANT CULTURES

MARK
GRIFFIN
&
THERON
WALKER

Brazos Press
A Division of Baker Book House Co
Grand Rapids, Michigan 49516

Published by Brazos Press
a division of Baker Book House Company
P.O. Box 6287, Grand Rapids, MI 49516-6287
www.brazospress.com

Printed in the United States of America

Library of Congress Cataloging-in-Publication Data
Griffin, Mark, 1962–
    Living on the borders : what the church can learn from ethnic immigrant cultures / Mark Griffin and Theron Walker.
        p.   cm.
    Includes bibliographical references.
    ISBN 1-58743-066-5 (pbk.)
    1. Christianity and culture—United States. 2. Immigrants—United States—Social life and customs. I. Walker, Theron, 1967– II. Title.
    BR517.G75 2004
    261'.0973—dc22   2003018222

Contents

Introduction

At the northern edge of Oklahoma City's sprawling metropolitan area, motorists are greeted by the sight of a giant cross. It towers above the interstate and the new housing developments stark and chalk-white, like a gleaming monument. At 137 feet in height the cross jostles with water towers and grain elevators for dominance of the skyline. A motorist coming in from Wichita can see it for miles across the rolling prairie-woodland. It is still at some remove—on the outer borders—of that familiar corridor of billboards and signs (fast-food chains, motel chains, gas stations) that tells our motorist that she could be anywhere—or nowhere in particular.

A sign indicates that this cross-on-the-plains belongs to Life Church, one of the metropolitan area's nondenominational megachurches. It is not to everyone's liking. To be sure, ethnic festivals and old cathedrals are more colorful and attractive forms of religious expression. And it is difficult to resist negative comments about the suburban sprawl that it portends. And yet this gleaming pillar has a curious appeal to it. The cross is a welcome relief from that plastic forest of commerce up ahead, which assaults the eye with too much stimulus. It stands at an oblique remove from the global culture of consumption that Benjamin Barber has labeled *McWorld*: ". . . a busy portrait of onrushing economic, technological, and ecological forces that demand integration and uniformity and that mesmerize peoples everywhere with fast music, fast computers and fast food—MTV, MacIntosh and McDonald's—pressing nations into one homogeneous, global theme park."[1]

And, as it happens, there is more to this Life Church cross of Edmond, Oklahoma, than meets the eye. It would take more than a passing glance to know that it was erected around the same time that the image of the cross was removed from Edmond's city seal; that this suburb's logo has a blank spot, which the cross once occupied. If our motorist chanced to see a police car or had occasion to drive past the municipal buildings, her eye would be sure to gravitate to that curious blank quadrant of the seal. She might notice the other more "neutral" symbols that remain on the logo: a covered wagon, the clock tower at the local college.

She would notice that even the Bible Belt isn't what it used to be. She would have just been welcomed to our local region of post-Christian America.

The Melting Pot

If America can be described as a "melting pot,"[2] then it seems quite obvious that the church has now become part of the stew, jostling for prominence with everything else in the pot, tossed to and fro in this marketplace of lifestyles, cultures, and merchandise. Stripped of its official status, the church cannot claim to be "above" the cultural process that for decades, or centuries, has been melting down all other subcultures that have deviated from its norm.

It is no secret that the melting pot into which all cultures have been expected to dissolve is not culture-neutral.[3] The basic ingredients from the beginning were from European-American (or "white") cultures that enjoyed the unique privilege of not being considering *ethnic*. Ethnic cultures are supposed to lose their flavor and just fit into the old recipe. Melting-pot culture is symbolized (more and more, it seems) by shopping malls and MTV—rather than churches, synagogues, and town squares. The standard definition of the *melting pot* is "a place where immigrants of different cultures or races form an integrated society."[4] While accurate enough, this definition fails to register the corrosive experience of cultural loss for many immigrants, and, in increasing numbers, Christians.

J. Hector St. John de Crèvecoeur (1735–1813) is not neutral when he talks about the melting pot. His 1782 *Letters from an American Farmer* is the design for the melting pot. "He is an American, who, leaving behind him all his ancient prejudices and manners, receives new ones from the new life he has embraced. . . . Here individuals of all nations are melted into a new race of men."[5] The promise of an integrated, new race sounds friendly enough. But having one's way of life treated as *prejudice* that must be left behind is no pleasant experience.

Obviously, people come to and stay in North America because it has so much to offer. As de Crèvecoeur said, "*Ubi panis ibi patria*," meaning, "Where there is bread, there is one's fatherland."[6] Immigrants and Christians alike enjoy the freedom and openness of this society. Many, however, fail to see the hidden cost of membership in this "new race of men." The melting pot is a place devoted to the creation of a uniform national culture in which communal traditions are exchanged for consumer choices. The melting pot is an American flag fluttering over malls and car dealerships—with the cross out on the edge of normal sight. As de Crèvecoeur gleefully concluded, "thus all sects are mixed as well as all nations; thus religious indifference is imperceptibly disseminated from one end of the continent to the other."[7]

Our first major assumption is that *Christians now find themselves in the melting pot, as many an ethnic immigrant.*

Melting-Pot Liberalism

The myth, or ideal, of the melting pot is a particular American incarnation of "liberalism." In broad terms, liberalism is the tradition that favors the freedom of individuals to act or express themselves in a manner of their own choosing, and which grants an ultimate status to the freely choosing individual.[8] Liberalism is the box that contains both Republicans and Democrats—Reagan and the Bushes no less than the Kennedys. It is tolerant of all that can be defended as a matter of private, individual choice. Liberalism subtly pushes people into separating their private lives from their public lives, their actions from their beliefs, their life as citizens from their culture. Liberalism welcomes all cultures, nationalities, and religions as ingredients and, to its credit, grants them an unprecedented amount of freedom. Nevertheless, like all systems or regimes, its toleration is never absolute. Pretending to be a neutral principle or procedure that dispenses with the baggage of the ethnic past, melting-pot liberalism is bound to be an appealing model at a time of terrorism and ethnic strife. And yet we are reminded by immigrant narratives that stripping the person of his communal bonds in the name of individualism, assimilation, and progress can breed its own share of strife; at the bare minimum, it exacts an expensive psychological toll.[9]

Liberalism is not a neutral procedure or process. Like the emperor with no clothes, liberalism pretends to be neutral and unbiased, but in fact promotes a particular agenda and a particular conception of the good. There is no such thing as a set of unbiased principles that Christians or members of any other culture must answer to.

Kenneth Craycraft argues in *The American Myth of Religious Freedom* that liberal toleration is meted out in lesser portions to those who appeal to communal obligations and authorities as the basis for their opinions; it is reserved in full portions for those who appeal to private, individual choice.[10] A Catholic who quotes a papal encyclical will not experience the same degree of religious toleration as the Protestant whose religious language is private and unmediated by communal rituals and authorities.

Christians are discovering, as the melting pot enters its secular, post-Christian phase, a fact that ethnic immigrants have lived with for a long time: Cultures are tolerated as long as they remember what is fit for public consumption and what must remain at home. Jews experienced the intolerance of liberalism as far back as 1789 in France. "It is necessary to refuse everything to the Jews as a nation and grant the Jews everything as individuals," said Count Stanislas de Clermont-Tonnerre.[11] The door to free societies is open to those who will "surrender their collective identity in exchange for full rights as individual citizens."[12]

The gradual process of secularization removed the church's exemption from the heat of the melting pot. The day that prayer was sent home from school (domesticated in a literal sense) was not the beginning of secularization, but the beginning of the end. And now the Nativity scene has been moved from the town center of little Hamburg, New York, where Theron grew up, to the front lawn of one of the churches. Our traditions are tolerated as long as we don't assert their presence in public. So it's tolerable to celebrate Christmas at home, but manger scenes are to be kept off of public lawns. Santa, of course, is welcome everywhere. (Now *there's* something to give one pause.) Liberal toleration is thus confined to realms that bear the name "private": the private sphere, the private sector.

A bumper sticker in Colorado Springs (where Theron now lives) is quite telling. In a place renowned for being the headquarters of Focus on the Family, motorists are treated to the bumper stickers demanding: "Focus on your own damn family." In other words, "You keep marriage your way, and I'll keep it—or not—my way." How, in the land of the free, are you supposed to respond to the accusation that you are "interfering" with an individual's "freely chosen" lifestyle?

Our concern here is not the ways in which liberalism grants people "too much freedom," but the subtle and unexpected ways in which it allows freedom to be truncated and circumscribed. America has been tolerant (to a fault) of all those forms of violence that Pope John Paul II includes under the rubric of "the culture of death." But it has been much less accommodating toward those who practice peaceful forms of radical dissent—like the Indian tribe in Oregon that wants to use peyote in its religious ceremonies, or the fundamentalist mother who does not want her children learning about evolution. This concern with the limits of liberal tolerance has pointed us in the direction of public intellectuals (like Benjamin Barber, Michael Sandel, and Alasdair MacIntyre) who do not seek to standardize the political as a game of autonomous individuals and "neutral" procedures.

Liberalism is the box that we are trying to think outside of. We describe our efforts as "postliberal" rather than "antiliberal." We are interested in an order in which liberalism is not the commanding "emperor" of all other traditions, but a fellow competitor who can be engaged in dialogue—and whose strengths and weaknesses as a tradition can be assessed. Our second major assumption follows: *the melting pot is much less benign than it appears to be, and is not a good thing for the church or ethnic minorities.*

The Cracking Melting Pot

The melting pot is in trouble. With all the jostling around, the different melting points of the ingredients, and the uneven distribution of heat, the pot developed some cracks. America is commonly spoken of as a "fragmented" nation. The fault lines run along the familiar race, class, gender, religious, and ethnic boundaries. The melting pot has proven a messier, more uneven process than its architects predicted it would be.

The problem, for starters, is the recipe. Instead of being one single stew, the melting pot has been from its inception bi-layered: a white layer (like New England clam chowder) above and a darker-colored layer (like New Orleans gumbo) at the bottom. Puerto Rican actor/activist Ben Soto must have something like this in mind when he says, "The melting pot is a dangerous place, really. You don't bubble up to the surface; you just settle like sludge at the bottom."[13]

African-American history, which intersects at some points with the experiences of recent immigrants, has been a steady program of exclusion. This junction is visible in Piri Thomas's 1967 memoir, *Down These Mean Streets.* Thomas is a black "Newyorican" (New York resident of Puerto Rican descent), who as a young man did everything he could to fit into the American melting pot of the late 1950s. After a painful rejection from the mainstream, he fell in with a criminal crowd. Thomas's story is all too typical.

The Civil Rights movement managed to shake the situation up a bit—earning for a fraction of those at the bottom of the racial caste system unprecedented access to the melting pot proper. But the overall picture of a segregated nation with "people of color" concentrated in the inner cities remained more or less the same. Those left behind in the "barrios" or "ghettos" saw their neighborhoods decline as their most talented citizens moved to the suburbs, which were, and remain, the locus of the melting pot. There are oases of urban revitalization that make one hopeful, but the general feeling is that the barrios are still places to be "gotten out of," places that breed contempt—or self-contempt—among those who do not get out.[14] The term *barrio* is respectable in Latin America, while in the United States it's obviously derogatory. At best a way station for the unassimilated masses, the barrio is a place that self-respecting immigrants, or at least their children, are supposed to leave.[15]

The contrast between the dreams of the Civil Rights movement and the grim realities of life in decaying urban neighborhoods gave rise to both despair and ethnic separatist movements, such as the Nation of Islam. These movements contribute to the sense that we live in a fragmented world. These recent cultural developments seem to have brought our post-Babel condition into sharper relief than ever before.

Benjamin Barber argues that we are locked in a downward-spiraling dialectic of *Jihad vs. McWorld*. *McWorld* represents the tidal wave of uniformity that is washing away all distinctions. *Jihad* represents militant, dogmatic, and violent particularism. The jihad impulse may begin with an innocent desire to maintain a local identity "against the numbing and neutering uniformities of industrial modernization and the colonizing culture of *McWorld*."[16]

Our world, for quite some time, as Barber sees it, has been undergoing a process of re-tribalization that feeds on the globalization that it is reacting against. The forces resisting assimilation into global markets and the national melting pot are as different and as varied as can be imagined, but they all oppose McWorld. "Caught between Babel and Disneyland, the planet is falling precipitously apart and coming reluctantly together at the very same moment."[17]

The most traditional "tribalists" are peaceful, even pacifist—like the Amish. At the other extreme, there are militant ethnic/fundamentalist organizations that, since the national trauma of September 11, 2001 (and April 29, 1995, the day of the Oklahoma City bombing), we are all too aware of. These militants are what first springs to mind when the word *jihad* is uttered.

We owe much to Barber's analysis of our polarized nation/world and the surprising interdependence of the two polarities of *McWorld* and *Jihad*. However, we have strong reservations about Barber's use and application of the term *jihad*. The fact that he categorizes all re-tribalization groups under this term (Hasidic Jews and the "religious right" no less than "Serb assassins" and "neo-Nazis") is objectionable for two reasons. First, it pathologizes any group—however peaceful —that resists the melting-down process in the name of the particular. Second, it fails to do justice to the term *jihad* itself, which in mainstream

Islam suggests something more akin to "resistance" than to "terror." Symbolic use of militant language and actual violence are not the same thing. Violent and peaceful resistance are not the same thing. If all forms of resistance were homogenized with the stigma of violence, then a trip to Disneyland would be tantamount to consorting with Revelation's whore of Babylon.

There are some cultural enclaves that are devoted neither to peace nor to violence. Some evangelicals and charismatics, for example, draw sharp, dualistic lines between themselves and a corrupt "world." Ironically, while condemning the world, these dualists are connected to McWorld through subterranean passages. It's just odd to see those who reject the world as *evil* through and through embracing lavish styles of consumption as true faith; or others who argue for a hermetically sealed intellectual system built on the "objective facts" of the Bible; or still others who call evangelism the building of churches to entertain, and ministry addressing people's "felt needs." Dualistic Christians symbolically employ the language of warfare, crusades, and fortresses even as they eat from McWorld's menu. As we will note in chapter 3, this Christian subculture has an ethnic analogue in the Cuban exile culture of Miami, where lavish consumption and the theme of exile have a paradoxical coexistence.

College campuses are another kind of ghetto. Students spout sentences like, "You wouldn't understand; it's a Chicano/Chicana thing," and label as "sell-outs" those who do not conform to some political litmus test. Richard Rodriguez and Linda Chavez, two prominent Latino defenders of assimilation, have had plenty of encounters with hostile college audiences. They like to call this expression of identity politics "illiberal multiculturalism." This phenomenon is no doubt real, though it has been overplayed in the polarized debate concerning college curricula. It is the unintended consequence of liberal multiculturalism—whose ultimate objective is not ghettoization but a slower process of assimilation.

Then, of course, there is the neglected, decaying urban neighborhood that most associate with the word *ghetto*. In Spanish, it might be referred to as the *barrio*—the term used in Linda Chavez's *Out of the Barrio*. The walls around this ghetto have been constructed from the outside by exclusion and neglect. Those same walls have often been reinforced by self-contempt from within. But even here, McWorld has come a-courting through the back door. Music born of the despair of the ghetto is marketed in the suburbs as part of an adolescent culture of rebellion. Most ghettos are related to McWorld in complex, unexpected ways. The relationship is not just one of polar opposition but one of startling and sometimes explosive symbioses. "Ironically, a world that is coming together pop culturally and commercially is a world whose discrete subnational ethnic and religious and racial parts are also far more in evidence, in no small part as a reaction to McWorld."[18]

Our third major assumption is that *the "ghetto" or "barrio" is a much more complex phenomenon than it appears to be, but it's not a suitable alternative to McWorld.*

Rallying to Save the Melting Pot: Fast-Track and Multicultural Liberalism

One reaction to the fragmented melting pot contends that the "heat needs to be turned up": government programs should be cut and "hyphenated" identities that retard assimilation should be discouraged. *Fast-track liberalism* argues for a sink-or-swim approach that forces the immigrant to adapt as soon as possible to life in an English-speaking, consumer-oriented culture. Whatever cultural tradition immigrants bring with them is a matter for the "private sphere" or the "private sector."

There is a rough correspondence between this group and those who lie politically right of center. Most advocates of this position would refer to themselves as conservative, neo-conservative, or libertarian—though the view is held by a smaller number of left-of-center liberals.[19] We label the position *fast-track liberal-*

ism because it is a form of modern individualism advocating the quickest possible assimilation of cultural minorities into the national melting pot. Linda Chavez (a leading Hispanic neo-conservative) and Richard Rodriguez (a writer of a more libertarian bent) are the figures we will focus on who articulate this position.

Multicultural or *slow-track liberalism* advocates a kinder, gentler melting pot. Multiculturalists would "turn down the heat" of the melting pot to prevent it from breaking apart. Slow-track liberals are often accused of promoting fragmentation and separatism. However, assimilation is still their goal; they just have a longer timetable. Multiculturalism produces a spicier, more colorful monoculture, but a monoculture nevertheless. Though this movement is often referred to as "multicultural liberalism" or just plain "liberalism," its ultimate aim is not diversity. Multiculturalism is all too often nothing more than a monoculture in which one can choose, buffet-style, from a host of "lifestyle options" that have been lifted out of their communal settings and packaged for consumption.[20]

Most slow-track multiculturalists are on the political left, but as in the case of their not-so-distant cousins, the fast-track liberals, this too is a generalization. Cuban-American writer/critic Gustavo Pérez Firmat, who coined the phrase "living on the hyphen," espouses a right-wing anti-Castro politics. Slow-track multiculturalism is a form of modern individualism that seeks a slower process of assimilation, often with the help of government funds. Multiculturalists fall somewhere between strong assimilationists and separatists, but in the end, everyone is thrown into classical liberalism's melting pot.

Into the Melting Pot

In the United States, it's been easy for Christians to think of the faith as an "idea," and not as a way of life. The church has been one of the major players in American history. In the colonial era, many saw North America as "the promised land." The Americas were a new world, a second Garden of Eden. Many came for the sake of religious freedom, which meant the ability to do Christianity *their* way. Even when church and state were formally separated by the Bill of Rights, "everyone" assumed the United States would be a "Christian nation." This new republic was, after all, ordained by God. There was an implicit promise that Christianity was fully at home in America.

For better or for worse, few would disagree that since the 1960s, the church has ceased to be the agent drawing the lines of inclusion for our society. Up until the latter part of the twentieth century, Christians (Protestants in particular) were the "spoon" stirring the melting pot: controlling immigration, education, and government; praying in school and in Congress; defining the moral vision and ethos of America.

Now, alas, the spoon has fallen into the pot and is caught up in the stew with all the other ingredients. It clangs against the walls of the pot, sometimes calling more attention to itself now than when it was doing the stirring. Sometimes it takes on the shrill clamor of bitter demagogues; sometimes it whines for attention like an irritating child; sometimes it becomes a freakish hybrid of snake-oil salesman, talk-show host, and conspiracy theorist.

The noise can also sound like the rhetoric of a love-hate relationship. American Christians in a post-Christian nation are reeling in confusion over how the words *American* and *Christian* go together. On the one hand, many feel deeply connected to this nation. Christians proudly assert that America has solved the church-state issue. Christians boast that religious freedom is at the heart of the American experience, and that this is the place where you are free to practice your religion without government interference or control. They are inclined to regard the melting pot as an image of everything that is wonderful about America.

On the other hand, the same Christians have bitter words for all of those things that seem to define a nation that has turned its back on them: a set of public values too "thin" to prevent moral decline and a laissez-faire consumer culture run amok. There is fear at the news of school and sniper shootings. There is indignation at the signs and billboards that advertise not just gasoline and fast food, but diverse forms of "adult entertainment"—bodies marketed as merchandise. There is a sense of betrayal at the Supreme Court's drift from upholding the church's cherished values to shedding them like so much unfashionable clothing.

In some quarters there is a desire to return to the Constantinian melting pot of yesteryear. We use the term *Constantinian* here to refer to an era in which the church served as "chaplain to the nation," and thus enjoyed a "hegemonic" status of official favor. It refers to a time in which the church was Uncle Sam's most favored stirring-spoon. For the same reasons that post-Constantinian theologians have articulated, we take "retrenchment" to be neither feasible nor desirable.[21]

Life after Babel

Our postmodern situation is often compared to Babel.[22] Western Christian civilization is coming apart at the seams. The received ideas about truth, beauty, and the good have been replaced by pluralism. The melting-pot image itself has been discarded in many circles as a relic of the imperialistic past. The culture wars are summed up in images that suggest the aftermath of Babel, that is, confusion. Even though the image of the melting pot has been discarded by many and replaced with terms like *mosaic, symphony,* or *salad,* the drive toward a monoculture lives on. *McWorld* is its name.

Immigrants unmask North American assumptions about the world. They are the needed "control group" that the modern experiment of "mass-techno-liberal-capitalism"[23] must account for. Immigrants from non-Western cultures come to America with traditions that, by definition, clash with the life-ways of the West. Traditional cultures know little of liberalism's separation of values from facts, of private from public, of faith from politics. Immigrants expose North American Christians to the fact that American culture and Christianity are not one and the same.

The church, as an ingredient in the melting pot, faces the same threat of cultural disintegration that immigrants face. Even the most grateful-to-be-here immigrants of the first and second generation always carry with them a longing for home and a feeling that they will always be foreigners, consigned to the margins of the dominant culture. American Christians are now "resident aliens" in the land of their birth.

Becoming an ingredient in the melting pot has caused Christians to question liberalism. The heat of assimilation has made Christians see that discipleship is more than holding the "right" opinions in a Christian nation; it is belonging to a particular *polis* called "Church." When the church lost control over melting-pot liberalism, Christians began to realize that the gospel creates a culture, a "holy nation" (1 Peter 2:9) that cannot simply be part of the melting pot's "new race of men."

Our fourth major assumption is that *Christians and ethnic immigrants face the same challenge. Both must navigate between the twin perils of ghettoization and absorption into "McWorld" via the melting pot.*

The irony for Christians is that they *ever* considered a particular civilization their homeland. A careful reading of the story of Babel reveals something quite different from the common understanding of what Babel represents.[24] In Genesis 11, we learn that the "whole earth had one language." People gathered on a plain, and said to one another, "Come, let us build ourselves a city, and a tower with its top in the heavens, and let us make a name for ourselves, lest we be scattered abroad upon the face of the whole earth." They started their project, and then received a building inspection from the Lord. The Lord confused their speech so they could not communicate. The Lord's goal was to limit what they could do. *Babel* is the name their abandoned city came to be known by; it is translated as "confused."

Some background may be helpful. By chapter 11 of Genesis, the expulsion from the garden and the flood had already happened. Nevertheless, the Lord's purposes for creation were still moving ahead. The Lord willed that the people should fill the earth (Gen. 1:28). They were supposed to be "spread abroad" (10:18). Scattering was not part of the curse; it was a blessing, the increasing and multiplication of every kind and of the union of male and female. But scattering was the very thing the people on the plain of Shinar feared.

The city and its tower represent a covenant to create unity, but God is not a participant in the covenant. God does will unity, but it is the unity of each kind, according to its own, in covenant obedience with the Lord. We assume that the confusing of language was a *curse;* it was actually the means to restore God's sovereign will and blessing. We could read the story as a critique of all attempts to create a monoculture! Modern liberalism is, in this light, a "Tower of Babel Project."

The church can no longer serve as engineers for the Babel project. As children of Abraham, Christians are called to be sojourners in each and every land, culture, and epoch. "A sojourner in a society stands somewhere between the native-born person and the complete foreigner, a resident alien who has no permanent possession or natural rights in the place in which she or he dwells."[25] It is high time for the church to remember, with St. Augustine, that "there is a city of God, and its Founder has inspired us with a love which makes us covet its citizenship."[26] Perhaps one of the best descriptions of the sojourning church is found in "The Epistle to Diognetus":

> The Christians are not distinguished from the rest of mankind either in locality or in speech or in customs. For they dwell not

somewhere in cities of their own, neither do they use some different language, nor practice an extraordinary kind of life. . . . But while they dwell in cities of Greeks and barbarians as the lot of each is cast, and follow the native customs in dress and food and the other arrangements of life, yet the constitution of their own citizenship, which they set forth, is marvelous, and confessedly contradicts expectation. They dwell in their own countries, but only as sojourners; they bear their share in all things as citizens, and they endure all hardships as strangers. Every foreign country is a fatherland to them, and every fatherland is foreign.[27]

The very idea of *sojourner* is that of a new race, united not under the banner of liberal democracy,[28] but by the grace of the shed blood of Christ Jesus (Eph. 2:11–22).[29] Consequently, it became common in the New Testament and beyond to address letters saying, "To the exiles of the Dispersion . . ." (1 Peter 1:1) or "The Church of God which sojourneth at Smyrna to the Church of God which sojourneth in Philomelium and to all the brotherhoods of the holy and universal Church sojourning in every place . . . (Letter of the Smyrnans).[30]

We hope to acquaint the church with its neighbors who live on the borderlands (both literal and figurative) of the United States. Besides the injunction to "love the sojourner" (Deut. 10:19), these neighbors can be prophets to the American church —voices in the wilderness or voices outside of what is so easily taken for granted. They show Christians what it means to be "exiles of the dispersion." They remind the church that this earthly city in which we dwell, as wonderful as it may be, is not the heavenly city (Heb. 13:14). They reacquaint us with our pilgrim heritage as children of Abraham. We must hear their stories, because we Christians are called to be "insider-outsiders"[31] (Heb. 13:13) in this land—given that "our citizenship is in heaven" (Phil. 3:20).

This stance is by no means one of passive resignation. We are calling for cultural engagement, but an engagement that always recognizes that all civilizations are passing. While seeking a more vigorous public role, the church should find common cause with immigrant cultures that share an interest in promoting a postindividualistic national ethos. Before all distinctive communities fade into the mix, and before we fall into a McWorld dystopia along the lines of Huxley's *Brave New World*, the church must call all principalities and powers into question (Eph. 6:12), even while affirming the essential goodness of the created order. The church should not reassert itself in some commercial or official guise, but should embrace this frontier, borderland space that the times have thrust upon it. From this insider-outsider location the church can best resist the corrosive pressures of the melting pot and the consumer culture that follows in its wake. The church's mission is to be carried out from this vantage point. It is a location that implies neither complete withdrawal from the "world" of political power, of getting and spending, nor a bid to be at the commanding heights of that world. The church's finest hours are always at the borderlands of nations and empires, not at their centers. Our fifth major assumption is that *the Church should seek a role that is vigorous and public, but not one that is official or hegemonic. Our citizenship is in heaven.*

A Word of Clarification

We are concerned with the common status of the church and immigrant minorities, but we should be clear about what we are not saying. Both groups share the same social space, but they do not deserve equal allegiance. For the Christian, the church and, above all, God, deserve an allegiance that far transcends the allegiance we owe to either the nation-state or the ethnic group. We are even hesitant to place allegiance to the ethnic groups over allegiance to the state; both are capable of eliciting idolatrous (and sometimes barbarous) allegiances and should at best serve as checks and balances against each other—human nature being what it is.

But even though ecclesial and ethnic cultures do not belong to the same orders of allegiance, the two groups do have enough in common to warrant studying them in conjunction. Both face an identical set of pressures: to be domesticated, privatized, and assimilated. Both are at their best when they resist these pressures and express themselves through associations that stand between the individual and the state but are not part of the "private sector" of commerce. Both are at their best when they have a public presence that seeks neither a dominant political position nor a market-oriented, corporate alliance. Both are at their best when they inhabit the nation's borderlands or their own revitalized plazas: spaces that are historically rooted and engaged with the culture at large; spaces vital enough to nourish and retain the younger generations.

To recap, then, we ask our readers to accept a set of five working assumptions—however much these might challenge conventional wisdom:

1. Christians now find themselves in the melting pot, like many an ethnic immigrant.
2. The melting pot is much less benign than it appears to be, and it is not a good thing for the church or ethnic minorities.
3. The ghetto or barrio is much more complex than it appears to be, but is not a suitable alternative to McWorld.
4. Christians and ethnic immigrants face the same challenge. Both must navigate between the twin perils of ghettoization and absorption into McWorld via the melting pot.
5. The church should seek a role that is vigorous and public, but not one that is official or hegemonic. Our citizenship is in heaven.

Overview

We will envision the space that lies between the ghetto and McWorld by bringing together the work of culturally engaged theologians, social scientists, and philosophers who seek to move beyond the ethos of modern individualism, as well as the work of some of America's finest first- and second-generation immigrant writers. In keeping with our focus on literature, we will offer not propositions or programs but concrete images and embodied, living impressions: fiestas and pilgrimages (chapter 1); traditions (chapter 2); bridges and diasporas (chapter 3); communities (chapter 4); plazas and borderlands (chapter 5); and communal authorities (chapter 6). These images and concepts are interwoven and interpenetrating throughout, like the threads that make up author Sandra Cisneros's caramelo-colored shawl. Central to these notions is that of the border/borderland.

The time frame we are looking at is the last three decades or so (from the aftermath of the 1960s to the present) and includes works ranging from Chaim Potok's *The Chosen* (1967) and Rudolfo Anaya's *Bless Me, Ultima* (1972) to Cisneros's *Caramelo* (2002). Our special focus is on the experience of Latinos—even though we devote some space to the Jewish-American novelist Chaim Potok and hope that our ideas can be suggestive to those studying other "ethnic" literatures. Aside from the fact that Latino cultures have experienced something of a renaissance during the last two decades, these also mark the site of a special interface between the ecclesial experience (Roman Catholic, for the most part) and the ethnic-immigrant one.

Chapter 1 deals with what we have defined as "fast-track liberalism" and devotes special attention to the San Francisco–based writer Richard Rodriguez. We focus on his defense of fast-track assimilation, its undeniable benefits as well as its offsetting psychological costs. We also look at how his writing converges with and diverges from that of Mexico's Nobel laureate, Octavio Paz.

Chapter 2 uses a historical and theological camera-focus to vindicate the concept of "tradition" as an indispensable and inescapable navigational tool. The gospel itself is a kind of tradition, as is the Enlightenment Project. In exposing the latter as a tradition-among-others, we point to the role of John Locke and Ralph Waldo Emerson in shaping the thought of writers like Rodriguez.

Chapter 3 emphasizes writers from the East Coast, especially Miami and New York. Gustavo Pérez Firmat, Oscar Hijuelos, Cristina Garcia, and Julia Alvarez are multicultural-liberal writers of Spanish-speaking Caribbean origin who think of themselves as living "on the hyphen." The hyphen that some of these writers speak of promises to enrich American culture and make it more of a genuine hybrid, but it is incapable of sustaining communal traditions over the long term. This is because the long-term effect of the hyphen is to give immigrant cultures a longer shelf life, not to sustain their communal bases. If living on the hyphen is an attempt to get beyond the polarities of the ghetto and McWorld, then it must be judged a dead end.

Chapter 4 examines the way contemporary culture destroys community. The late Chaim Potok, who articulates the Jewish-American experience, was a crucial figure, because he was the first major writer whose characters went against the grain of the melting pot. His characters engage in complex and painful negotiations with both the "secular-humanist" culture at large and the ghetto of Hasidic Judaism. In the process, Potok's novels deepen our understanding of communities and communal authorities.

Chapter 5 looks at to the borderland region of the Southwest, focusing on Rudolfo Anaya, Gloria Anzaldúa, Virgilio Elizondo, and Sandra Cisneros. We make the case for viewing the church as a "rooted diaspora" and a "borderlands" culture.

Chapter 6 uses historical and theological resources to examine the question of communal authorities. We will ponder these questions: What does it mean to be free? Is all authority essentially oppressive? Can we have community or receive traditions without personal embodiments of those ways of life?

A Sojourner's View after September 11

The Life Church cross of Edmond, Oklahoma, could be read as an outraged call to arms, a *jihad* to win back Christendom. On this reading, it would be championed by the right and feared by the left. Others might see it as one more commercial sign, one more billboard. But our reading calls for reflection rather than fear, outrage, or jaded skepticism. We propose that it be seen as a symbol of the church in a post-Christian era. It points to the fact that the church can have a vital role in public life (perhaps even a more vital role) while divested of the last trappings of official ties.

Our motorist who has driven past the Life Church cross will want to stop, if she has not been here before, at the Oklahoma Bombing Memorial, which honors the victims of the April 19, 1995, attack and lies a few blocks north of the downtown area. Run by the National Park Service, it has the polished, official aura of government war memorials. It speaks an abstract language of hope; the reflective surface of its still water and its golden portals (representing the moments before and after the blast) stand in stoical defiance of terrorism and hatred. It is a reminder, as if any were needed, that the values of this nation-state (tolerance and the rule of law, for example) cannot just be brushed aside as platitudes. Since the much more devastating attack of September 11, these values have proven effective in rallying people across the nation and the globe against terrorism—if not always in favor of the United States' particular response to it.

On the other hand, one suspects that the language of this monument is too abstract to speak to our deepest hopes and fears or to provide true meaning and lasting sustenance for the soul. One suspects that, over the long haul, we will need much more than stoic calls to return to the business of getting and spending. The statue of the weeping Jesus, erected by the Old St. Joseph Catholic Church across the street, must come closer to capturing the sentiment of those who survived the terror. The grief of this statue, whose back is turned to the scene of the crime, seems so much better poised to connect with people. The official monument—in all of its elegant Euclidian reserve—has no room for crosses or tears.

Our motorist will spare at least a thought (she cannot help but do so at a place like this) for the nation that now knows the scourge of terrorism. America's self-interest, in this post–September 11 world, consists in winning over communities whose values are "thicker" and much more historically rooted than those embodied in its spare monuments. Its self-preservation consists in cultivating alliances with ancient communities in places like Afghanistan—with people who will not be won over by the language of uprooted individualism and international corporations. America has a need, both at home and abroad, to be hospitable to these sorts of communities.

From this site, one need not look too far to feel the vital flavor of communities that are still distinctive. To the north and the south, there are oases of urban revitalization in an area that was once a declining and semi-abandoned area: Asian shops and restaurants off N.W. 23rd Street; Mexican murals, bakeries, and tortilla shops on S.W. 25th Street. These latter neighborhoods have enough of a Hispanic population to sustain distinctive practices and lifeways. These barrios, which are beginning to show signs of revitalization, are like cultural outposts or colonies of the U.S./Mexico borderlands region, which lies a few hundred miles to the south.

What all of these "ethnic" neighborhoods have in common with the statue of the weeping Jesus, and even the Life Church cross, is that they inhabit a region distinct from fast-food chains and abstract principles. The church, like these communities, lies now at an oblique remove from government buildings and corporate headquarters. In that vital remove lies its mission to thrive and better connect with its own cultural wellsprings.

The fate of the church, in short, is part and parcel of everything that is particular. For this reason alone, if for no other, Christian sojourners can benefit from a dialogue with recent immigrants and their "ethnic passages."

1

Of Triumphs without Fiestas

Richard Rodriguez's
Labyrinth of Solitude

A campaign of retribution" was the phrase Linda Chavez used to describe her failed cabinet nomination on January 9, 2001. She added, in her withdrawal of her bid for a post in the newly elected George W. Bush administration, that her (Democratic) critics were engaged in an "effort to continue the election by other means." A newspaper article of January 9 explained that she withdrew her name after questions arose concerning an illegal immigrant who had stayed with her and performed household help in the early 1990s.[1]

Anyone who knows the least bit about Chavez's career as a public intellectual cannot miss the ironies of this event. Here was the author of a book titled *Out of the Barrio: Toward a New Politics of Hispanic Assimilation,* now being hounded by those same ethnic ties that she had urged her fellow Latinos to put behind them. Having made a career of combining the admonitions of Laura Schlessinger ("Get over it!") and Gloria Estefan ("Stand up and make it happen!"), she was now calling attention to her "victim" status. She was complaining how unfair it was that the president-elect had sailed through his DUI allegations, while a much less serious charge had torpedoed her career, and of how the Republican leadership had let her nomination wither and die by telling her to keep silent. Having downplayed her ethnic roots and criticized those who made too much of an issue of them, she was now being held back by a charitable indiscretion (helping a Hispanic illegal immigrant in need) that had everything to do with those roots. She had argued for advancement through personal initiative, as opposed to group entitlement. Group affiliations, she had insisted, were to be confined to the private margins of one's life.

And now her communal ties would not remain on the margins.

What is one to make of these communal identities that so often come back to claim us, knocking on our doors, interrupting the geometric solitude of our suburban lawns like oddly dressed evangelists, or like villagers in their colorful peasant attire? What is one to make of these emissaries of some half-forgotten past? They come calling us to allegiances more solid, more substantial than the fabric of the Stars and Stripes or the language of Emerson or the lure of shopping malls. They invite us to embarrassment, to dissent, perhaps even to law-bending behavior. How are we to respond to their claims on our roots amid a culture fashioned for uprooted individuals?

Perhaps some version of these questions passed through Chavez's mind as she went through her botched nomination process. Or perhaps not, judging by her comments and her recently published memoir.[2] But we find them unavoidable, at any rate. And in spite of the fact that this news flash now looks like a trivial footnote in light of the events of September 11 and its aftermath, we view it as significant for the enduring questions it raises—questions that will be with us long after the showdowns with Al-Qaeda and Iraq have come and gone. It raises questions about what America is and is becoming. It raises questions about an America that is projecting itself around the world and, now more than ever, needs to win over as allies people who are rooted in ancient communities—people who have an instinctive suspicion of America's uprooted individualism.

We are putting Chavez's idea of old-fashioned melting-pot assimilation to the test. In other words, we are pitting her "fast-track liberalism" (more apt to be referred to in the American political context as "neo-conservatism") against her actual *experience* and against that of Richard Rodriguez, another formidable Latino defender of fast-track assimilation. In choosing Chavez and Rodriguez, we make our case that the "melting pot" is a bad idea by engaging some of its best and brightest defenders. We want to listen to those who have, to all appearances, succeeded in "melting" into the English-speaking mainstream. And what we discover when we listen to them is that the old melting-pot idea is harmful to even its most gifted advocates. As we will be noting in more detail, even though particular cultural heritages do not fare well in America over the long term, they are more resilient in the historical short term than many immigrants expect them to be.

We engage the writing of Richard Rodriguez to make three related points: (1) that the melting pot (even in the best of cases) is a much more tortuous and conflict-ridden process than its defenders assume; and (2) that assimilation and secularization are two sides of the same coin, two aspects of the same "leveling" cultural process. As a third major point we will also suggest, with references to Mexican Nobel laureate Octavio Paz, (3) that forces of resistance to this process include communal acts such as pilgrimages and festivals. Within these communal acts we begin to envision the space that lies between the ghetto and McWorld.

It would be difficult to find a better poster child for Linda Chavez's vision of fast-track out-of-the-barrio assimilation than Richard Rodriguez. The eloquence and insight of his memoir make it a good place to sort out both the strengths and (somewhat less apparent) shortcomings of her model. Few are more committed than Rodriguez to the central prescription of Chavez's book *Out of the Barrio:* success through educational achievement and a relegation of ethnic heritage to the private sphere. Rodriguez's *Hunger of Memory* (1982) is the tale of a Spanish-speaking boy who succeeded at Stanford and Cambridge, refusing to speak Spanish and renouncing the affirmative action programs that were offered to him as a Hispanic.

Rodriguez is most widely recognized as the essayist-commentator who has made frequent appearances on public television's *MacNeil/ Lehrer NewsHour* with short insightful essays.[3] His appearance is that of a dark-skinned Latin American, and his manner is that of the cosmopolitan intellectual: an eloquent iconoclast with a hint of world-weariness. One can hear in his writing and speaking the voices of Ralph Waldo Emerson, Walt Whitman, and (in a more ambiguous sense) Octavio Paz. Controversial political stances aside, his work manages to plough deep furrows in the soil of American literature. The meandering path of his thought is often difficult to follow. It is like a tortuous mountain trail that offers breathtaking vistas, switchbacks, and apparent reversals of direction. One theme prevails and remains constant, however: a commitment to a heroic brand of individualism and a total immersion in the American melting pot.

Alienation: The Cost of Melting In

In his essay "Aria"—the first of those that make up the book *Hunger of Memory*—Rodriguez describes the experiences and rationale that lie behind his opposition to bilingual education. As it was for all children in 1950s Sacramento, California, English was the sole public language of his education. His schooling took place under the tutelage of Irish nuns who subjected him to a total-immersion, sink-or-swim environment—and Rodriguez evinces gratitude for their "tough love":

> Fortunately my teachers were unsentimental about their responsibility. What they understood was that I needed to speak a public language. So their voices would search me out, asking me questions. Each time I'd hear them, I'd look up in surprise to see a nun's face frowning at me. I'd mumble, not really meaning to answer. The nun would insist, "Richard, stand up. Don't look at the floor. Speak up. Speak to the entire class, not just to me!"[4]

In contrast to English, Spanish was the charmed intimate language of home. It was meet and right that this be the case, for to bring it into the public arena (school) would have had the effect of trivializing it: "I hear them [supporters of bilingual education] and am forced to say no: it is not possible for a child—any child—ever to use his family's language in school. Not to understand this is to misunderstand the public uses of schooling and to trivialize the nature of intimate life—a family's 'language.'"[5] Behind the sacred, cloistered, and domestic walls of the home, Spanish could be protected from public misuse and abuse. "Bilingual enthusiasts, moreover, sin against intimacy. . . . Context could not be overruled. Context will always guard the realm of the intimate from public misuse."[6]

But, alas, English was not content to remain the lord of public life. English would, in time, invade even this hallowed domestic space, exiling Spanish from even the most intimate of exchanges. At the behest of the Irish nuns, Richard's parents began to speak English at home also. Public alienation was overcome at the high cost of private alienation: Richard's father retreated into silence, and his mother became an awkward participant in his domestic conversations. Spanish-speaking relatives began to refer to Richard as a *pocho*—a term for the over-Anglicized, soulless Mexican-American who has committed the opposite sin of that of the defiant ethnic militant. And his relatives had cause for concern. He found himself no longer able to speak Spanish, relegating it more and more to the status of a relic:

> But once I spoke English with ease, I came to feel guilty. (This guilt defied logic.) I felt like I had shattered the intimate bond that had once held the family close. This original sin against my family told whenever anyone addressed me in Spanish and I responded, confounded.[7]

But once again, Rodriguez is not airing a grievance here. His attitude remains, as ever, one of stoical gratitude, stoical acceptance of what he feels to be inevitable. Anything less than this private alienation (with all of its consequent grief and loss) would have meant in his view a public alienation, a slowing of his assimilation into America as a fully autonomous individual. This is Rodriguez at his most Emersonian, embracing the assumptions that, at least up until postmodern times, have held the American psyche in their vise grip.[8] Bilingual/bicultural education retards the process—to the point of being "fatal" or "dangerous" —by keeping these ties on an artificial life-support system. "Just as Spanish would have been a dangerous language for me to have used at the start of my education, so black English would be a dangerous language to use in the schooling of teenagers for whom it reinforces feelings of public separateness."[9]

Rodriguez's argument here is much more all-embracing (and of more far-reaching significance) than a debate about government funds for this or that program. When he states that particular group ties reinforce "feelings of public separateness," he is saying that group identification as such (unless that group is made up of mainstream, English-speaking individualists) is inimical to one's participation in the American experience. This assumption is the more fatal one—at least to someone who is interested in the survival and well-being of anything that is particular and communal. It runs counter to the need, for which we will argue, for an ethos in which the appeal to communal bonds is plausible. Assimilation, melting-pot style, comes with a high price tag for Rodriguez: alienation from hearth and home.

Domestication for the Sake of the Nation: The Common Experience of the Church and Ethnic Immigrants

Even more significant than this phenomenon of alienation is the fact that Rodriguez's Christian faith (he is a member of the Roman Catholic Church) and his ethnic/linguistic heritage are subjected to the same process of privatization and marginalization; his Roman Catholic heritage and his ethnic Spanish-speaking heritage both undergo a process that we will call domestication for the sake of the nation. This comes as no surprise, if one accepts the notion that the church is a culture (often overlapping but never identical with ethnic culture).[10]

Rodriguez speaks as a liberal Catholic (at least at this stage of his life) lamenting the loss of his faith's public role, but with a resigned acceptance that this is a fair price to pay for the freedom and autonomous choice he enjoys as a U.S. citizen.

> When I go to church on Sunday I am forced to recognize a great deal about myself. I would rather go to a high ceremonial mass, reap for an hour or two its communal assurance. The sentimental solution would be ideal: to remain a liberal Catholic and to worship at a traditional mass. But now that I no longer live as a Catholic in a Catholic world, I cannot expect the liturgy—which reflects and cultivates my faith—to remain what it was.[11]

He refers to the loss of his faith's public and communal status as a process of "Protestantization." Protestantism, as he sees it, is better adapted to the ethos of liberal individualism—which involves approaching God alone and keeping one's faith to oneself:

My own Catholic Church has in recent years become more like a Protestant Church. Perhaps Protestants will teach Catholics like me how to remain believers when the sense one has for so much of one's day is of being alone in faith.[12]

This cultural stance means domestication in both senses of the word: as confinement to the private sphere (designated since the nineteenth century as the woman's domain) and as a process of taming, of purging "wild" and unassimilable elements.

A radical critique of this process of domestication can be found in Kenneth Craycraft's recent book *The American Myth of Religious Freedom,* mentioned in our introduction as a book that shines a harsh spotlight on the limits to religious freedom in America's classically liberal regime. Craycraft would cast Rodriguez (at least at present) as someone who has bought into a distorted and trun-cated form of freedom—one tailored to the needs of the liberal order, not the needs of his faith. The "Protestantization" that Rodriguez accepts signals his willingness to defend his Roman Catholic commitments only as a matter of lifestyle choice, not as a matter of communal allegiance and obligation. It is a dimin-ished concept of religious freedom that even Protestants of all stripes have come to chafe at. For it is true, as Craycraft would argue, that we are members of traditions not of our own choos-ing and making; that our most cherished convictions are not arrived at in isolation from church communities and traditional authorities; that freedom is always a relative thing, meted out in stale and watered-down portions to those who are not willing to regard themselves as uprooted individuals.[13]

If we fast-forward about fifteen years in Rodriguez's life to his second collection of essays, *Days of Obligation: An Argument with My Mexican Father,* we find Rodriguez also chafing under the concept of individualistic freedom he had earlier seemed to wear so well. The fact of the matter is that almost two decades after the publication of *Hunger of Memory,* and after two decades of domesticated Catholicism, we find him railing like a prophet against his own church's loss of a communal ethos, and against the loneliness that he feels. The domestication of his faith, like the domestication of his mother tongue, has exacted its usual toll: loneliness. The prosperous and monolingual neighborhoods of the American Dream can seem, all too often, like labyrinths of solitude.

Rodriguez's solitude is best depicted in his transcription of an exchange that he has with a group of priests at a retreat, in which he chides them for pandering to a consumer-driven multiculturalism whose ethos he rightly identifies as a new-and-improved brand of individualism:

> I have no agenda, Father. I am not a priest, I have no Prescription, I have no intention. I am lonely. I tell you I see the disintegration of Catholicism in America and I tell you the Catholic Church does not attend to the paradox of American Catholic lives. We confess a communal faith; we live in an individualistic culture.
>
> Look, here we are—Catholics—arguing about multicultural-ism while secular America and even evangelical Protestantism take lessons from our tradition. Environmentalists, for example, question the wisdom of unbridled individualism.
>
> Environmentalists claim the enlightened imperative of a We. As Latin America turns Protestant, North America experiences the dawning of a Catholic vision—the "globavillage"—an ecology closer to medievalism than to the Industrial Age.[14]

This sounds, on the face of it, like a much different Rodri-guez—one closer to Craycraft, or to communitarian public intel-lectuals such as Robert Bellah. But his quarrel with individual-ism is, all along, a lover's quarrel or a psalmist's lament, and the communitarian yearnings he expresses are a brief departure from the overall pattern of his thought. The meandering course of his thought allows him to engage in a kind of dialogue with his Mexican roots and to express longing for a more commu-nally rooted existence. But the heroic individualism that he is committed to must pull him back toward the promised land of the melting pot, away from the "Egypt" of his ethnic past. For someone who is as steeped in the language of Emerson as Rodriguez is, Mexico draws him with an irresistible force but repels him with a stronger one.

Of Pilgrimages, Diasporas, and Festivals: The Short-Term Persistence of Ethnic Consciousness

Days of Obligation speaks in large measure of a return to Mexico—of a series of (somewhat reluctant) pilgrimages to the land of Rodriguez's roots. One senses in this book an effort to reconnect to those roots, even though he seems to do it with an ultimate reserve and skepticism, and holds Mexican nationalism at arm's length. The title of his first book (*Hunger of Memory*) seemed to go against the grain of the book's assimilationist message; but now, in this later collection, there truly seems to be an insatiable "hunger of memory" at work. Pilgrimages to Mexico are not what we would have expected of a fully assimilated Emersonian individual—which Rodriguez had seemed to be on the path to becoming. Speaking of a film project in which he is involved, he states, "A man who spent so many years with his back turned to Mexico. Now I am to introduce Mexico to a European audience."[15]

Such is the case with Rodriguez. He comes back to Mexico because he is a U.S. citizen who is part of Mexico's "diaspora north of the Rio Grande"—to borrow a phrase from Jewish-Mexican-American writer Ilan Stavans.[16] He knows he is a part of that network of expatriates, émigrés, and children of émigrés concentrated in cities like Los Angeles, San Francisco, Houston, and Chicago.

He returns as a reluctant, alienated, and subversive pilgrim. Even if his reason is to put to rest the presence of Mexico (and of a Mexican-American ethnic consciousness) in his life, he must do this. Even if he intends to take the switchback trail that goes in the opposite direction from ancestral rootedness, he is drawn back.

His skeptical brilliance is nowhere better on display than in the essay "Mexico's Children," in which he combines anecdotes from his travels south of the border with a description of Mexico—the "motherland"—as a passive-aggressive maternal presence. Mexico, he argues, tightens her grip from afar with the language of blame, betrayal, and wounded pride. "The government of hurt pride is not above political drag. The government of Mexico impersonates the intimate genius of matriarchy in order to justify a political stranglehold."[17]

But it is also true (and Rodriguez must give credit where it is due) that the same government has served as a protective advocate of her émigrés and citizens abroad. He remembers how Mexican consulates in California stood up for all people of Mexican descent who were singled out for abuse or discrimination. "Her protective arm extended not only to the Mexican nationals working in the U.S., but to the larger number of Mexican-Americans as well. Mexico was not interested in passports; Mexico was interested in blood."[18] She represents remembrance in a land of individual liberties and disregard for the past. "Never to be outdone, Mother Mexico has got herself up in goddess cloth. She carries a torch, too, and it is the torch of memory. She is searching for her lost children."[19] Mother Mexico enters Richard's life as one of those emissaries in peasant attire who makes a surreal appearance on the streets of the American Dream; she bears the torch (or perhaps the festival incense) of memory. And he is compelled at last to enter into dialogue with "Mexico's Children," to weigh in on some of the issues that Mexican writers, artists, and politicians have grappled with.

Those of us who were born and raised in Mexico (like Mark, who now lives in Oklahoma) are aware of the two major leitmotifs that have always dominated the discussion of Mexican culture: (1) the nation's *mestizaje* (its hybrid blend of "Indianness" and "Spanishness"); and (2) the nation's frustrated attempts at progress and the realization of its ideals (from the 1810–1821 War of Independence to the 1910–1920 Mexican Revolution). Mexican schoolchildren know the anthems to the heroes of Mexico's revolutions (always drawn in the ennobling aesthetic of the French Revolution) and the special holidays devoted to the honoring of the nation's mixed-racial heritage (El Día de la Raza). Those of us who spent our childhoods in Mexico are bound to be all ears when Rodriguez (a California-born Mexican-American) weighs in on these matters.

As expected, Rodriguez has his own subversive and meandering spin to offer. His first essay in *Days of Obligation* (which bears the deliberately misleading title "India") sets out to reclaim the term *Indian* from both the American New Ager and the Mexican nationalist. He rejects the notion (common in New Age circles) of the Indian as a special being with mystical ties to nature. And he also rejects the Mexican-nationalist myth of a grand Arcadian Aztec civilization that was ended by the "fall" that was the Spanish conquest. The Indian, to Rodriguez, is neither a nature guru nor a tragic hero. He (or she, for that matter) is an active agent who *chose* to become Catholic, to absorb European culture in its Spanish guise, and, when the situation demanded it, to exchange Spanish for English.

It is testimony to Rodriguez's subversive rhetorical brilliance that he is able to take one of the most nationalistic of Mexican concepts and claim it for his own individualistic vision. The Aztec (Mexico's national symbol) is now an English-speaking, dark-skinned, postmodern Catholic—no less Catholic than the Celts and Iberians who were Christianized in the waning days of the Roman Empire. His heroism is exhibited not in his cultural resistance, but in his wholehearted embrace of the English-speaking melting pot.

In his most recent book, *Brown*, this subversive imperative continues with even greater force. Again, the title of the book is deliberately misleading. This is a work that signals not so much the embrace of a "brown" ethnic heritage (as in the 1970s

Chicano-movement phrase "Brown is Beautiful") as the embrace of all that is "impure," of unresolved contradiction, of that which undermines the notion of racial and ethnic identities altogether. "I write about race in America in hopes of undermining the notion of race in America."[20] The term *brown* is to be understood not so much in contrast to other racial/ethnic groups, but in contrast to the "puritan" strain that Rodriguez sees as permeating American culture, insisting that one be pure and authentic in one's allegiances, suspicious of all that is theatrical and paradoxical:

> But there was also something un-American in the Puritans' insistence upon a deathless identity once here. For America would turn out to be a land of inventors and self-inventors, a land of imposture. The theatrical possibilities of America would extend to blackface and feathers. Insofar as America would become an anti-Puritan country, Americans would dream of becoming other than they were. Insofar as America would remain a Puritan country, theatricality would meet the accusation of "inauthenticity." What is at stake in all this is the nature of authenticity, which is the Puritan dilemma.[21]

Rodriguez's Mexican interlocutor in this whole discussion of "brownness" is the essayist José Vasconcelos, and his 1925 essay *La raza cósmica* [The Cosmic Race]. Vasconcelos, the force behind the public works of Mexican muralists such as Diego Rivera, argued that Mexico's distinctiveness as a nation lay in its racial/cultural mixture—and that this fact was to be its source of ethnic/national pride. It is, once again, testimony to Rodriguez's rhetorical skill that he is able to take a concept like *mestizaje*, so identified with Latin-American ethnic consciousness, and turn it into a symbol of individualistic defiance of all racial/ethnic categories.

Rodriguez also weighs in on the question of Mexico's numerous revolutions and the course of human affairs in general. Throughout *Days of Obligation,* he draws a sharp distinction between the "comic" outlook of the Protestant "North" and

the "tragic" outlook of the Latin/Mediterranean "South." And
he believes, like his (Mexican) father, that "much in life is failure or compromise." His views on the tragic are like bookends
that open and close this second collection of essays, and are a
shorthand way of describing his own "Augustinian" approach
to historical questions:

> The comedy of California was constructed on a Protestant faith
> in individualism. Whereas Mexico knew tragedy. My Mexican
> father, as his father before him, believed that old men knew
> more than young men; that life will break your heart; that death
> finally is the vantage point from which life must be seen. I think
> now that Mexico has been the happier place for being a country
> of tragedy. Tragic cultures serve up better food than optimistic
> cultures; tragic cultures have sweeter children, more opulent fu-
> nerals. In tragic cultures, one does not bear the solitary burden
> of optimism. California is such a sad place, really—a state where
> children run away from parents, a state of pale beer, and young
> old women, and divorced husbands living alone in condos.[22]

In this venture into the arguments that concern Mexico and its
"diaspora," he has something of a mentor in Octavio Paz. Paz's
stature as Mexico's late official poet laureate belies the extent to
which he made a name for himself critiquing Mexican nationalism (along with all forms of authoritarian rule). For example,
Paz shares with Rodriguez the view that the national myth of
an Edenic Aztec civilization destroyed by evil Spaniards with
the help of an oppressive Catholic Church owes much more to
the spirit of the French Revolution than to anything Aztec. Both
writers share the view that this "anticlerical" picture does justice
to neither the popular religious practices of most of the population nor the extent to which Mexicans (and Mexican-Americans)
are heirs to the culture of Spain. Besides having these affinities,
Paz is also the consummate cosmopolitan who has spent much
of his time outside Mexico as an expatriate writer and diplomat
(first in the United States, later in Paris, Tokyo, and New Delhi).

His essayistic masterpiece, *The Labyrinth of Solitude,* is as much about the modern condition of uprootedness, as much about the Mexican émigré or wandering expatriate, as it is about Mexican character itself.[23]

In addition to sharing Rodriguez's views on "Indianness," Paz shares his skepticism regarding historical matters—and on the course of human affairs in general. One might characterize the debate among Mexican artists/intellectuals as pitting those of an anticlerical/Marxist bent (epitomized by Diego Rivera and his grand, officially sponsored murals) against those of a more skeptical (and non-Marxist) bent. Paz belongs to the second camp. His rejection of Marxism has not driven him to embrace liberalism (the other great modern myth of progress), but something more akin to communitarianism or classical republicanism. His thought is rooted in the tradition of Emiliano Zapata, leader of a peasant agrarian movement that sought a return of communal lands (known as *ejidos*). For Paz, Zapata's legacy is not the proto-Marxism that Diego Rivera depicts it to be, but a "return" to a communal landownership that had been one of the more benign features of the Spanish colonial order.[24] Though not an order he would wish to emulate, the colonial system was in some ways preferable (for the Indian) to the brutal period of modernization that followed (and was carried out under the banner of liberalism and progress). Paz is no less "Arcadian" than many of his contemporaries, but he does not equate the prelapsarian state with any particular civilization (Aztec, Maya, or otherwise), and he is more willing than his nationalist contemporaries to see the good as well as the bad in the Spanish colonial period. "This utopian, communitarian concept, I find it among (colonial-era) missionaries and also in Zapatism. I do not find it in liberalism, which is utopianism in the rationalistic sense of the word. Most revolutions in the twentieth century have been like the liberal Mexican revolution in the nineteenth century: attempts to impose geometric patterns upon living realities."[25]

The writers share these strong affinities on this issue of "Indianness," even though Rodriguez never quite embraces Paz's communitarianism. We can also picture them as being in agreement concerning the (optimistic, "comic") myth of the American Dream—America's utopian version of the myth of liberal progress. Paz is skeptical of false hopes endemic to places like the United States and of its embrace of "continuous, unlimited progress"—in keeping with his ambiguous approach to the modern era. "The history of Spain and her former colonies, from the sixteenth century onward, is the history of an ambiguous approach—attraction and repulsion—to the modern era."[26]

Paz also seems to be behind Rodriguez's comments about Latin culture being a festive culture, in spite of (or better yet, because of) its "tragic" sense of life. Paz speaks of this "tragic" sense of life as an embrace and transcendence of "solitude." The Mexican's sense of "solitude" (a sense of a lost Eden, of alienation from a state-before-the-fall) is felt at the communal level and transcended in the communal ritual of the festival. The solitary Mexican loves fiestas and public gatherings.

> Any occasion for getting together will serve, any pretext stop the flow of time and commemorate men and events with festivals and ceremonies. We are a ritual people, and this characteristic enriches both our imaginations and our sensibilities, which are equally sharp and alert. The art of the fiesta has been debased almost everywhere else, but not in Mexico. There are few places in the world where it is possible to take part in a spectacle like our great religious fiestas with their violent primary colors, their bizarre costumes and dances, their fireworks and ceremonies, and their inexhaustible welter of surprises: the fruit, candy, toys and other objects sold on these days in the plazas and open-air markets.[27]

The (North) American, on the other hand, chooses to go it alone and never finds the exit from the labyrinth of solitude. Believing the world to be "perfectible" through work and himself to be "purifiable" through it, he continues to be alienated and alone. "But now he cannot recognize himself in his inhuman objects, nor in his fellows. . . . He is alone among his works, lost . . . in a 'wilderness of mirrors.'"[28]

This also goes, of course, for the uprooted Mexican (Paz refers to him as the *pachuco*) who wishes to forgo his past and go it alone. Inside the melting pot is a vast, geometric labyrinth of solitude.

The Brown Summit of Heroic Individualism

Rodriguez's engagement with Mexico's leading voices is profound, but it ends with a parting of the ways. His communitarian yearnings remain at the level of tantalizing hints and partial forays, never going in new directions. And this is understandable: to follow them through to their logical conclusion would mean a complete about-face, a complete break with the stances staked out in 1982 in *Hunger of Memory*. The most important guiding assumption of that first work—that all forms of culture should remain confined to the private sphere—remains unchallenged.

For Rodriguez, it comes to this in the final analysis: instead of following Paz all the way down the mountain of modern individualism, he heads back up it. He heads for the summit of heroic self-reliance—there to be in the company of Emerson, Locke, Jefferson, and, of course, Whitman.

> I write of brown as complete freedom of substance and narrative. I extol impurity. . . . It is that brown faculty I uphold by attempting to write brownly. And I defy anyone who tries to unblend me or say what is appropriate to my voice. You will often find brown in this book as the cement between leaves of paradox.[29]

Insofar as this "brownness" is an embrace of contradiction and a refusal of the "puritan" impulse to place allegiances in some order, it is individualism (of a conflict-ridden, radically postmodern sort) that he gives us in the end. "When you slice an avocado, the pit has to go with one side or the other, doesn't it? Weighting one side or the other. A question about the authenticity of the soul, I suppose. . . . The tension I have come to depend on. That is what I mean by brown."[30] Like Whitman's poetic speaker, he holds all "creeds" and communal allegiances "in abeyance," the better to preserve his status as an autonomous individual, undefined by any of these things.

Enshrined on this cultural Mt. Rushmore of the American melting pot are the likes of John Locke, Emerson, Jefferson, William James, Whitman . . . and *in potentia,* Rodriguez himself. It is the communion of those who, at the deepest level, disavow communion and tradition. The view from here is anticlimactic. Instead of being vast, open spaces, the promised land below is paved over with suburbs and shopping malls, with flags fluttering over car dealerships. The august, monumental figures who have left behind the Egypt of ethnic tribalism also keep an elite, aesthetic distance over the new spaces they have cleared a path for. The labyrinths of solitude below are what come out of leaving the past behind—a labor they have pioneered.

So, for the moment, there remains for Rodriguez no exit from the labyrinth, no public festival to join. He remains resolute in what one reviewer describes in these terms: "He shuns the pack, rides alone. He writes a lonely line of individualism, the grandeur and grief of the American soul."[31]

A fine assessment, but is so much grief necessary? Is it necessary to leave the "barrio" to become a first-class citizen? Are there no options between the extremes of "puritanism" and the worldview of those divided, uprooted individuals who hold all creeds "in abeyance"? And as for the church, does it have no other alternatives beyond a "puritan" ghettoization that shuts out the "world" and a live-and-let-live relativism that reduces its faith to irrelevance? We hope not, of course, and have assumed the existence of a vital, alternative space.

Conclusion: Domestication and the "Christ *of* Culture"

What the experience of Richard Rodriguez shows us is that putting the nation and the individual first has the effect of *domesticating* our ancestral cultures (whether ethnic or ecclesial) and consigning them to irrelevance. Far from delivering on the freedom and emancipation that it promises, modern individualism confines us to privatized cultures and "labyrinths of solitude."

Within the life of the church, a parallel mindset is to be found. The analogue to Rodriguez's submission to the ethos of self-reliant individualism is what H. Richard Niebuhr refers to as the "Christ *of* Culture"[32] paradigm, which has, since the time of the Gnostic Christians, subordinated the faith to the dominant ethos of the nation or the empire: "So they harmonize Christ and culture, not without excision, of course, from New Testament and social custom, of stubbornly discordant features."[33] In the American context, this "Christ of culture" shares with fast-track assimilationism an (over)eagerness to harmonize ancestral tradition with the antitraditional tradition called melting-pot liberalism. This effort at harmonization leads, of course, to the ecclesial/ethnic tradition's subordination and ultimate irrelevance.

It is a false freedom indeed that asks us to relinquish or "privatize" our faith (and/or ancestral ties) in its name. So it is fitting that the following chapter, which sets out to vindicate tradition as a "life-giving vine," should turn first to the notion of "freedom." In it, we will also give some attention to the often invisible "tradition of disavowing tradition," whose pantheon Rodriguez seeks to join: to its origins, and to its stark opposition to the classical Christian tradition.

2

Tradition

Shackle of the Past or Life-Giving Vine?

Whoso would be a man must be a nonconformist. . . . Nothing is at last sacred but the integrity of your own mind. I remember an answer which when quite young, I was prompted to make to a valued adviser who was wont to importune me with the dear old doctrines of the church. On my saying, What have I to do with the sacredness of traditions, if I live wholly from within? my friend suggested,—"But these impulses may be from below, not from above." I replied, "They do not seem to me to be such; but if I am the Devil's child, I will live then from the Devil." No law can be sacred to me but that of my nature.

Ralph Waldo Emerson, "Self-Reliance"

This passage from Emerson's famous 1841 essay "Self-Reliance" is a paean to the new gods, the enlightened, liberated individuals. "Self-Reliance" is an argument about what it means to be human, and especially about what it means to be free. Western culture is built on the foundation of *freedom*. Freedom has different meanings in different cultures. *Which* freedom is Western culture founded upon? W*ho* formed the rationality for this particular understanding of freedom?[1]

Emerson thought of freedom as his right to be the judge of truth, without regard to tradition, authority, or community. Freedom is noninterference with an individual's thoughts, speech, beliefs, associations, or actions—as long as no one else's rights to the same are hindered. This rationality is displayed in full force in the Colorado Springs bumper sticker ("Focus on Your Own Damn Family") that we referred to in the introduction.

This rationality for freedom is a central tenet of the Enlightenment Project. For anyone in the West, this kind of freedom is self-evident truth. The Enlightenment Project leaders, as we said in the last chapter, make up an ideological Mt. Rushmore. René Descartes and John Locke gave us the theory, Thomas Jefferson wrote it into law, and William James turned it into a theology. Richard Rodriguez has tried to conform himself to their images.

Freedom "Enlightenment style" does not sit well with immigrants from non-Western cultures. Parents from the Old World are unfamiliar with our self-evident truth. They assume that their children owe them honor. They assume family loyalty. They come to America for freedom from poverty and tyranny. They expect opportunity, especially for their children. They are surprised when their children no longer keep the family traditions.

Traditions dissolve in the melting pot. Ironically, non-Western cultures are so appealing and interesting to Americans *because of* their traditions. Their holidays, foods, and social arrangements have color and flavor because they do not fit on the interstate's strip malls. The popularity of the film *My Big Fat Greek Wedding* surprised everyone.[2] It portrays family ties as something both to escape from and to embrace. These ties can neither be accepted as they are nor rejected wholesale. The Greek family in the film is appealing and thick in an ordinary kind of way. In our lonely, dislocated culture, old-world communal bonds and traditions look like a fairy tale.

Immigrants come to America seeking freedom. But the American dream becomes a kind of nightmare when their children want to be free just like the kids at school. People come to Christianity seeking freedom of another kind—freedom from sin and death; freedom to live in right relationship with God. Immigrants and Christians are aliens because they do not define freedom as self-reliance.

Let us look more deeply into our long-standing antipathy toward tradition. We will use the popular musical *Fiddler on the Roof* as an extended metaphor that helps us understand the Enlightenment tradition of destroying tradition. We will then look at the surprising comeback of the concept of tradition as an essential ingredient in all forms of thought. Next, we will examine the concept of tradition in the New Testament and in the life of the church in the first and second centuries. Finally, we will show that freedom cannot be had either when tradition is given divine, unchanging status or when it is absolutely rejected in principle. Tradition is an essential navigational tool for would-be sojourners.

The Destruction of Tradition

The musical *Fiddler on the Roof* [3] dramatizes Americans' double-mindedness toward tradition. On the one hand, we are drawn to tradition because it carries meaning, belonging, and the glue that makes a people a people. And yet, almost at the same time, we have a strange phobia about it. Tradition is what holds people back, we say, keeps them doing the same stupid things over and over, and Balkanizes cultures. Tradition represents the shackles of the Old World. The Frenchman St. John de Crèvecoeur described the ideal American as "leaving behind him all his ancient prejudices and manners" in order to be "melted into a new race of men."[4] Uncle Sam is the crotchety guardian of the melting pot, with little patience for tradition.

Fiddler on the Roof is interesting and vivid because of the rabbis, superstitions, foods, matchmakers, black clothes, and klezmer music. The story takes us, the audience, and transports us to a rich world so different from our own. For a couple of hours, we sojourn in a living tradition, a culture with soul. But we are, remember, a double-minded audience. *Fiddler* is about the *death* of a tradition. We also enjoy watching the destruction of this "odd" way of life.

Fiddler, like *My Big Fat Greek Wedding*, was a surprise success. Sholom Aleichem had written a collection of stories about Hasidic life in Eastern Europe.[5] Those stories formed the setting, but not the plot, of *Fiddler*. Ironically, that setting, the ghettos of Eastern Europe, is so far away that no one notices what the musical is about. As Richard Altman said, "I don't know who finally made the discovery that the show was really about the disintegration of a whole way of life, but I do remember that it was a surprise to us all."[6]

Fiddler is really an American story set in a Jewish village. The destruction of tradition is depicted as a positive, inevitable, forward evolution. First one daughter gets around the matchmaker and marries for love, and then another follows suit. The story gathers momentum—well, perhaps change isn't so bad—and then one of the daughters falls in love with a Gentile. This is too much for the poor father, Tevye. Why can't this impulsive, old-fashioned patriarch see that the language of love is universal, that it trumps tradition? We all breathe a collective sigh of relief when Tevye relents and life moves forward.

If *Fiddler* were more honest, then at the moment when Tevye relents, the fiddler (who is a metaphor for the precariousness of tradition) would slip off the roof, or at least drop his fiddle and helplessly watch it smash on the ground. The musical could break out in a new song: "The Day the Music Died." Instead, it bids a sentimental farewell to the very tradition it seems to celebrate. Its ultimate message is a nostalgia-ridden embrace of the melting pot. "Sunrise, sunset . . . one season following another, laden with happiness and tears."

During seminary, Theron had the privilege of taking a course on Judaism under Jack Moline, a local rabbi. Toward the end of the course, after winning the class's trust and admiration, Rabbi Moline brought up the touchy subject of intermarriage between Jews and Gentiles. "If I have persuaded you to care for and respect Jews," he said, "then I beg you not to do intermarriages. Nothing is more destructive to Jews and Judaism than intermarriage." He went on to say that in all but the most extraordinary circumstances, intermarriage means the end of the *Jewishness* of the Jewish partner. He or she will no longer keep kosher; will no longer pray and worship; will not pass the faith on to the children. The Jewish partner might be subsumed into Christianity, but more likely, faith will slip into irrelevance.

Fiddler on the Roof, for all of its nostalgia, does not do justice to the loss involved in the disintegration of a tradition. The musical feels wistful, but the message is that tradition's death is merely collateral damage in a natural process. *Fiddler* is propaganda for melting-pot ideology; it joins the list of melting-pot tales that hark back to the Horatio Alger myth. Rabbi Moline is in a better position to do justice to this sense of loss, to describe the full force of the process we described in the last chapter. Assimilation and secularization are two sides of the same coin, two aspects of the same *leveling* cultural process.

Richard Rodriguez's story parallels *Fiddler on the Roof.* Rodriguez, however, is more forthcoming. He admits that his assimilation, melting-pot style, comes with the high cost of alienation from hearth and home. But he goes to great lengths to prove to us that the price is worth paying. He claims that his access to the public life of the nation at large is worth the loss of his family's Spanish-speaking subculture. He also depicts the process of assimilation as natural. Its "naturalness" stems from the assumption that it is the only way to move ahead, the only way to be educated, the only way to be *free*.

But Richard's relatives knew the American tradition had consumed him. He had become a *pocho*. If it is true that tradition is the soul of a culture, then it is also true in some sense that Richard had lost his soul. Tevye and Richard meet on a landscape that is heroic, mournful, and soulless.

Some "naturalized" immigrants try, as we've said, to assuage their melancholia through pilgrimages to the motherland. These trips are bittersweet for the first-generation parents and are often resented by the second-generation children. A common thread running through Rodriguez's later work and Julia Alvarez's *How the Garcia Girls Lost Their Accents* (to be discussed in the following chapter) is the pilgrimage. In the latter novel, the Garcia girls are acting out. They are becoming too American, so their parents ship them back to the Dominican Republic. There, they are not just supposed to learn certain values. They are supposed to get the soul of the tradition in them, which will change their behavior. Theirs is a strange sort of forced pilgrimage. Why must all of these pilgrims, willing and unwilling, return to the "old country" if freedom can be found here in America? They of course lack soul, and soul can be regained only in the places where traditions are living. Domesticated traditions are mere shadows of living ones.

These "resident aliens" show us that the American Dream is not quite as free as we imagine. The privatization of tradition supposedly protects traditions from assimilation. In reality, domestication is another name for assimilation. Underneath all this is an odd sort of claim: *Because the melting pot does not touch the realm of private rights, you can pursue whatever happiness you desire, and therefore, you are free.* In other words, the melting pot is not itself a tradition.

From its inception, the Enlightenment Project attempted to be free of tradition, even defined tradition as a shackle. Stephen Toulmin, in *Cosmopolis: The Hidden Agenda of Modernity*, tells the fascinating story of René Descartes. Descartes postulated a kind of certainty that transcended tradition, superstition, history, and place. He created a "formally 'rational' theory grounded on abstract, universal, timeless concepts."[7] All knowledge—scientific, moral, theological—was squeezed into a mathematical model. The sure and certain foundation for thought was the autonomous individual, summed up in his most famous phrase, "I think, therefore I am." Toulmin demonstrates that Descartes's theory of knowledge did not develop in a vacuum. The *cogito sum* is the result of a particular time, place, and intellectual tradition.

John Locke, for example, dealt with a similar situation in England. English intellectuals were worn out by the absolutisms of kings and Puritans. They were wrangling with the question, "What is freedom?" The answer that won the day was the liberal definition: noninterference. The theory is that the ultimate good for humanity is a matter of personal opinion. In place of a *common* definition of "the good," we are now supposed to live according to our personal values. One should never impose one's values on another because values must be chosen freely.

Morality, according to Locke, is supposed to be as Euclidian as our well-planned suburbs and public monuments—no tradition, culture, or religion required. Reason, unencumbered by tradition, custom, or context (supposedly) discovers objective, neutral principles that can be used to make universal and unbiased judgments. Reason lodges in the autonomous individual, free of tradition, custom, or context. To be human is to be a decision-making individual, not a member of any particular community or faith. Reason (again supposedly) tells us we are all created equal and therefore have rights. We have rights to life, liberty, and the pursuit of happiness. We have a right to do whatever we want to do, as long as it doesn't hurt anyone.

It was no accident that the Enlightenment Project bracketed religion out of public discourse and the wrangling of politics. The project falls apart if this definition of reality is questioned. John Locke wrote in *A Letter concerning Toleration* (1689), "I esteem it above all things necessary to distinguish exactly the business of civil government from that of religion, and to settle the just bounds that lie between the one and the other."

There are two key points to the theory that make the boundary between religion and government so clear. One, religion is an individual, inward, private choice one makes when persuaded by rational argument. True religion, says Locke, is tolerant, because true religion never imposes its "truth" on someone else. Truth resides not in traditions, authorities, or communities; truth resides in the individual "for every man is orthodox unto himself."[8] Two, government's provenance is public life. Government should concern itself only with property and the impartial execution of law. Naturally, a *true* Christian wouldn't want the government to impose his or her *dogma* on someone else, much less have the government sponsor any particular belief. Religion is about values. Government is about facts. So the boundary between church and state really "protects" the church from the coercive power of the state. We know this, of course, as the definition of freedom of religion.[9]

Thomas Jefferson wrote this theory into law. From Locke, Jefferson learned that freedom resides in an individual's rights. Government and church should be separated because to be free is to be free of the interference from others. The very notion of rights is one of the great novelties of the project. Because freedom means noninterference, we must have a private realm of rights that cannot be touched by outside authorities, tradition included. Jaroslav Pelikan writes:

> For tradition was to [Mr. Jefferson] chiefly a hindrance, not a help, in the enhancement of life, the protection of liberty, and the pursuit of happiness. The Jeffersonian was not confined by any particular tradition: he had sought to reform the Christian tradition, he had disavowed the humanist tradition, and he had set himself outside the English tradition. The past, through which other men had discovered human possibilities, was for him corrupt and dead.[10]

Ralph Waldo Emerson has been called the creator of American religion.[11] He traversed the fledgling nation for over thirty years, preaching his gospel of "the infinitude of the private man," the irrelevance of tradition, and immediate personal access to truth. His essays are condensed versions of his lectures.

"The American Scholar," Emerson's 1837 address to the Harvard Phi Beta Kappa Society, is often called "America's intellectual Declaration of Independence."[12] In it Emerson asks, "Why should not we have a poetry and philosophy of insight and not of tradition?"[13] He then goes on to say that "the world is nothing, the man is all; in yourself is the law of all nature, in yourself slumbers the whole of Reason; it is for you to know all; it is for you to dare all."[14]

In "Divinity School Address," a speech to graduates of Harvard Divinity School, Emerson preaches Transcendentalism. "In the soul then let the redemption be sought. Wherever a man comes, there comes revolution. The old is for slaves. When a man comes, all books are legible, all things transparent, all religions are forms. The true Christianity—a faith like Christ's in the infinitude of man is lost. . . . Let me admonish you, first of all, to go alone; to refuse the good models, even those which are sacred in the imagination of men, and dare to love God without mediator or veil. . . . Trust thyself; every heart vibrates to that iron string."[15]

William James turned Emerson's religion into a formal theology.[16] James also had to deal with Darwin. "Given the randomness of existence, man's religious faith is essentially his faith in the existence of an unseen order of some kind in which the riddles of the natural order may be found and explained."[17]

In the end, James untethered Christian language from its traditional meanings. As Cornel West puts it,

> Emerson founded this new American religion, but James, in rising to its defense, became its first theologian. James argued Christianity was a failure because it was undemocratic! The language

of the Christian tradition had to be converted into the logic of
individualism. James co-opted the language of traditional Christianity into democracy [which] is a kind of religion.[18]

American Christianity reflects the image painted by James.
This "Christianity" is promulgated by the highly educated, but
is simply assumed by the average citizen.

George Lindbeck calls this sort of thinking about religion
"experiential expressivism."[19] God is experienced by individuals in the most general way. Then, individuals devise rituals to
repeat that experience, or employ metaphors to talk about what
is basically unutterable and unknowable. Experiences of God
are all really the same, only differing in name. "All religions
are forms." We could say that in this theology, God is made of
Teflon, and we keep throwing our metaphors at God, but none
of them stick.[20] Lindbeck puts it this way:

> As we move into a culturally (even if not statistically) post-
> Christian period, however, increasing numbers of people regard
> all religions as possible sources of symbols to be used eclecti-
> cally in articulating, clarifying, and organizing the experiences
> of the inner self. Religions are seen as multiple suppliers of
> different forms of a single commodity needed for transcendent
> self-expression and self-realization.[21]

We can safely conclude, therefore, that Emerson is alive and
well in America today.

Because of the continuing militancy of religious differences in
the Balkans and the Holy Land, and certainly since September
11, many feel compelled to deny all religious particularity.[22]
Now perhaps more than ever, whether in the hallowed halls of
universities and seminaries or in a casual conversation with an
acquaintance, religion is acceptable if it is absolutely tolerant
and gives up any claims of particularity. Any judgments about
the truth of religion are tantamount to jihad.

The Resurgence of Tradition

In recent years, even as the "Teflon God" has grown in popularity, a growing number of philosophers, scientists, and theologians have asked deeply critical questions of what modernity has taken as "self-revealed" truth. "Give me where to stand, and I will move the earth," said Archimedes. These intellectuals have argued in one way or another that there is no place to stand where objective, universal knowledge can be had. Postmodernism, ironically perhaps—and often in spite of itself—has unbound tradition.

Jaroslav Pelikan's 1983 Jefferson Lecture in the Humanities, *The Vindication of Tradition,* is an elegant argument. Pelikan is a historian of Christian theology. He begins his lecture with a reflection on *Fiddler on the Roof.* The musical, he says, illustrates one reason why the task of teaching has become increasingly difficult. Students are not schooled in the intellectual tradition of our culture. They are the products of a "tradition" that disavows tradition; but it is meaningless to teach them to disavow a tradition they know nothing of. Ironically, the rediscovery of tradition has happened among the unlikeliest of groups—secular academics:

> These past several decades may have been a period during which the home, the community, the school, and the church have all declined gravely in their ability (or willingness) to transmit one or another constituent element of the tradition. But those very same years have also been a period in which humanistic scholarship in various fields has been rediscovering "tradition."[23]

As an aspiring scholar, Pelikan used the same basic method that has been used for the last few centuries (our antitradition tradition). He looked to the "great men" who *changed* things. History moved forward with a continual sloughing off of tradition, carried out by geniuses. Pelikan subscribed, for a long time, to the "genius" theory of evolution in the very form and argument employed by Emerson.

What Pelikan discovered, however, was that looking at geniuses as figures towering over their times does not do justice to them. Geniuses cannot be understood in isolation from their times and their communities, but must be seen as spokespeople for them.[24] Key figures in Christian history, such as Augustine of Hippo or Anselm of Canterbury, did not understand themselves as either being in isolation from or towering over their tradition. They did not see themselves as transcending tradition. They saw themselves as *extending* the tradition, as getting the tradition right in their circumstances. This attitude was not simply one of obedience or humility; it was factually accurate. The historian, therefore, cannot build accurate histories by studying individuals isolated from their traditions.

In the Jefferson Lecture, Pelikan has more in mind than proving a certain method's effectiveness for the doing of history. He hopes to vindicate tradition and re-enfranchise those who came before us. "Tradition is the living faith of the dead, tradition*ism* is the dead faith of the living."[25] He draws attention to our friend Emerson. *Emerson defined tradition as tyranny.* All tradition is the dead faith of the living. To be a "man" is to transcend tradition.[26] Pelikan agrees with Emerson's notion that tradition can be deadly. But that is the case only when tradition becomes an end in itself. The creative process of making music, for example, does not begin where tradition leaves off. Rather, a composer's work is a part of the river that is tradition.[27]

The Enlightenment Project sought to base all knowledge on "self-evident" ideas or "formal" axioms. In reality, there have been no such things. Scientists have adopted one explanatory system or paradigm, used it until it could no longer make sense of the data, and then dropped the paradigm for a new one.[28] This very description reveals the new method that has come to the fore. It embraces tradition, but with a kind of self-awareness unseen prior to the Enlightenment. This new, more modest view:

replaces axiom systems, which aspire to universal timeless validity, by paradigms, which are the creations of a given age or phase of Science. It also substitutes for the dream of a singular method, applied across the board, the fact of plural explanatory methods, each of which is limited in scope and lifetime.[29]

This new, more modest method found its way into theology. George Lindbeck developed what he calls a "cultural linguistic" model for understanding religions. Religion, Lindbeck reasons, is a kind of language or culture. Differing religions shape life in different ways. They have different goals and different virtues inherent in the reaching of their unique goals. Becoming religious is like "going native" or learning a language. It is a process of "interiorizing outlooks that others have created, and mastering skills that others have honed."[30]

Lindbeck's "cultural-linguistic" method grew out of liberalism's inability to provide a common framework for religious dialogue.[31] Lindbeck spent many years working at ecumenism. Essentially, he found that "experiential expressivism" (the Teflon God) did not further dialogue, but ended it. There can be no such thing as dialogue when we assume our words for the divine really do not mean anything. This move honors no one. It makes us all the same, and all equally clueless. The subtext of any such dialogue is, "We're both saying the same thing. You just don't know it yet. But when I'm done educating you, you will." The irony is overwhelming. In an effort to respect all "traditions," Teflon theology forces everyone into its Tower of Babel . . . a kind of Hotel California ("you can check out any time you like, but you can never leave").[32] The cultural-linguistic approach is effective because it actually helps conversation. Like John Courtney Murray reportedly said, "A good conversation doesn't start until we get to a disagreement."[33]

Alasdair MacIntyre is one of the titans in this conversation. In *After Virtue,* he argues that our current culture wars are a symptom of the Enlightenment Project. Tradition is at the heart of his argument. In short, the Enlightenment Project tried to do ethics without tradition. The project began with the rational, reasoning individual. When the individual proved to be not so rational, the basis for ethics shifted to emotion, with Nietzsche as its prophet.[34]

MacIntyre defines tradition as *a historically extended, socially embodied argument, and an argument in part precisely about the goods that constitute that tradition.*[35] Parsing out this definition, we observe that a tradition is an argument about the point of life, or "the good." That argument is more than an idea; it's a way of life, a whole sensibility about what it means to be human. This sensibility is lived out in all the institutions and social arrangements of the tradition—in other words, it is socially embodied. As a way of life, a tradition is naturally very specific about what a good life is, and about what virtues of character a person must possess to have a good life. And, of course, a tradition is no fad; it's a way of life passed down or "handed over" from one generation to the next, which is to say, histori- cally extended.

Tradition has been born again. This new incarnation differs from its pre-Enlightenment predecessor. No one is assuming old ways are all good ways. But tradition is not merely a shackle. Tradition is a reality that must be engaged for thought itself to occur.

The Church as a Tradition

Christianity is an argument about the meaning of life. Jesus summed up the whole of the Torah (Instruction): Love the Lord God with all of your heart, soul, and mind, and love your neighbor as yourself. Furthermore, the gospel (the good news) is what God has done in Christ. Where that story is proclaimed and experienced, the brokenhearted are healed, and the captives are set free.

The Enlightenment Project's argument about the meaning of life opposes that of Christianity. N. T. Wright claims that the most troubling issue with the Enlightenment is not its much publicized dualistic worldview, but its presentation of a rival argument about the meaning of life.

> The real problem with the Enlightenment is that it offered a rival eschatology to the Christian one. Christianity began with the thoroughly Jewish belief that world history was focused on a single geographical place and a single moment in time. The Jews assumed that their country, and their capital city, was the place in question, and that the time, though they didn't know quite when it would be, would be soon. The living God would defeat evil once and for all, and create a new world of peace and justice. The early Christians believed that this had in principle happened in and through Jesus of Nazareth. . . .With the Enlightenment . . . all that had gone before was a form of captivity, of darkness; now, at last, light and freedom had dawned. World history was finally brought to its climax, its real new beginning, not in Jerusalem, but in Western Europe and America. Not in the first century, but in the eighteenth.[36]

The church, through its sacraments and mission, bears witness to its argument about the meaning of life. Worship itself is first and foremost a witness to the truth of what God has done in the world through Christ. Worship is not meant to move us emotionally, though it can. Worship is not meant to be an environment in which unbelievers come to believe, though they can. Worship is not meant to be a source of inclusion, though it can be this too, and more besides. In worship, the church rehearses the story of God working out his providential purposes through Israel, becoming human in the person of Jesus, dying, rising, giving the Spirit to the church, and ascending. N. T. Wright says, "[The gospel] is not then, a system of how people get saved. The announcement of the gospel results in people being saved."[37]

The great theologian of Christian mission Lesslie Newbigin
claims that the basic task of the church is to be the bearer of
the gospel, or as we have put it here, God's argument about the
meaning of life:

> The church is the bearer to all the nations of a gospel that an-
> nounces the kingdom, the reign, and the sovereignty of God. It
> calls men and women to repent of their false loyalty to other
> powers, to become believers in the one true sovereignty, and so
> to become corporately a sign, instrument, and foretaste of that
> sovereignty of the one true and living God over all nature, all
> nations, and all human lives.[38]

The church's worship is supposed to embody the gospel.[39] Baptism, for example, is a form of worship in which people enter the
church. Baptism happens only once and takes little time. Yet
the whole of Christianity is summed up in it. In Romans 6:3–4,
St. Paul writes, "Do you not know that all of us who have been
baptized into Christ Jesus were baptized into his death? Therefore
we have been buried with him by baptism into death, so that, just
as Christ was raised from the dead by the glory of the Father, so
we too might walk in newness of life." The language of Romans
chapter 6 is one of dominion and allegiance. To be dead in our
sins is to be captive to a whole way of life, or tradition, that is at
odds with God. Baptism signifies dying to Satan, to the world,
and to sinful desires in us, that we might be raised with Christ.
Life in the Spirit is a life characterized by the fruit of the Spirit.
Love, joy, peace, patience, and the rest are the virtues of a life of
Christian love. These virtues are not simply new behaviors we
are supposed to pursue because God said so; they are intrinsic
qualities of the players in God's drama, or the citizens of God's
kingdom.

Holy Eucharist, or communion, is not just a meal that is
memorial of what Jesus did with his disciples the night before
he died for us. Holy Eucharist is a living reminder of the whole

gospel story, and of what it means to be a disciple of Jesus. In this feast of thanksgiving (the literal English meaning of the word *Eucharist*), we receive God's life, and we share our lives with the gathered community and with God. Eucharist embodies Christ's words "for whoever would save his life will lose it; and whoever loses his life for my sake and the gospel will save it. For what does it profit a man, to gain the whole world and forfeit his life?" (Mark 8:35–36). Christ gave his life for the world, and the Father vindicated him by raising him from the dead.[40]

Christians are supposed to shine as lights in all of their relations with the world. Christian life is supposed to enact God's argument about the meaning of the universe.[41] In his letter to the Philippians, St. Paul writes,

> Have this mind among yourselves, which is yours in Christ Jesus, who, though he was in the form of God, did not count equality with God a thing to be grasped, but emptied himself, taking the form of a servant, being born in the likeness of men. And being found in human form he humbled himself and became obedient unto death, even death on a cross. Therefore God has highly exalted him and bestowed on him the name which is above every name, that at the name of Jesus every knee should bow, in heaven and on earth and under the earth, and every tongue confess that Jesus Christ is Lord, to the glory of the Father. . . .
>
> Do all things without grumbling or questioning, that you may be blameless and innocent, children of God without blemish in the midst of a crooked and perverse generation, among whom you shine as lights in the world. (Phil. 2:5–11, 14–15)

All social relations, whether between husband and wife, parent and child, overseer and slave, or citizen and ruler, are understood within this basic framework.[42] The passages about the subjugation of women and of slaves are among the most difficult for Westerners. This is because *freedom* in the New Testament is not fundamentally considered to be an issue of social standing. Freedom is first and foremost an issue of knowing to whom we belong. Freedom is not so much about location in life; it's about truth. When enslaved to sin, the logic of Romans 6 argues, we are slaves of death. But when enslaved to God, we are in reality free, and so enjoy the gift of eternal life. Because of Christ, we are free and have basic dignity regardless of our situation. This is why the meek and the persecuted are counted privileged or blessed.

While the gospel does bring about physical liberation—the rich are cast down and the poor lifted up—it first wins the battle in hearts and minds. The concern of the various New Testament epistles is that, in their relations with one another and the world, Christians demonstrate the truthfulness of the hope in them. Civil Rights leaders such as Martin Luther King and Cesar Chavez were able to achieve concrete, legal equalities because they took for granted this basic human dignity in the sight of God.

In 1 Peter, the church is portrayed as a kind of priesthood of truth. Because God laid the foundation stone of Jesus Christ, Christians are built into a spiritual temple. We could think of that temple as the Temple of Truth. The common priesthood is the church's living demonstration of the truth. The ministry of this priesthood is a living demonstration that Jesus is who the church—husbands, wives, elders, slaves, and citizens—says he is. St. Peter writes:

> Now who is there to harm you if you are zealous for what is right? But even if you do suffer for righteousness' sake, you will be blessed. Have no fear of them, nor be troubled, but in your hearts reverence Christ as Lord. Always be prepared to make a defense to any one who call you to account for the hope that is in you, yet do it with gentleness and reverence; and keep your conscience clear, so that, when you are abused, those who revile your good behavior in Christ may be put to shame. (1 Peter 3:13–16)

In sum, core Christian beliefs are represented in the rituals or sacraments, especially baptism and Eucharist, which in turn provide the rationality for all Christian practices.[43]

Since the dawn of the Reformation, Protestants have held a deep antipathy toward tradition. Jaroslav Pelikan shows how, for the likes of Luther, tradition was like barnacles clinging to the church's ship; it was the stuff of "Popery." "Luther [was] summoning [his] contemporaries to move beyond tradition or behind tradition to authenticity: Tradition was relative and had been conditioned by history; Truth was absolute and had been preserved from historical corruption."[44] Where the Protestants of Luther's day claimed tradition was relative, Roman Catholics claimed it was revealed by Christ to his apostles. Tradition was a kind of parallel authority to Scripture, handed down from bishop to bishop.[45] Neither claim is exactly right. Rather than rely on these old Protestant and Roman Catholic assumptions, we will look at tradition in the New Testament and in the early church.

Jesus used the word *tradition* to mean unfaithful, willful, human innovation. In a disagreement with the Pharisees over ritual hand washing, Jesus said, "You leave the commandment of God, and hold fast the tradition of men" (Mark 7:8). Jesus himself and early Christianity were untraditional. Both rejected the time-honored and the ancient. Both rejected respected rival arguments about the meaning of life.

When St. Paul, for example, says in Colossians 2:8, "See to it that no one makes a prey of you by philosophy and empty deceit, according to human tradition, according to the elemental spirits of the universe, and not according to Christ," he's making two points. First, the Colossians should not buy into any rival accounts of the universe, because they are just that, rivals to the argument of the gospel. Second, the Colossians should not fall into the trap of buying into these truth claims just because they are old!

The New Testament is clear that Christians are not to live under the yoke of human traditions, but only under the gospel. But we must recognize the context of these statements. Unlike us, premoderns generally had a deep respect (often unquestioning) for ideas and ways of life that were old. Jews were generally considered strange in the Greco-Roman world, but they were tolerated because of the antiquity of their way of life. The early church was considered dangerous because of its novelty. Christians were considered superstitious by the Romans not because they believed unbelievable things, but because the content of Christianity was untraditional.[46] People in late antiquity trusted tradition. Today, we trust only what is new; or, in Emerson's words, "Trust thyself: every heart vibrates to that iron string. Accept the place the divine Providence has found for you; the society of your contemporaries, the connexion of events."[47]

But the concept of tradition is not always used in a negative sense in early Christianity. Tradition was authoritative even before the first pages of the New Testament were penned. In 1 Corinthians, St. Paul writes about right belief and practice around the Lord's Supper: "For I received from the Lord what I also delivered to you . . ." (11:23). At the very center of the church's worship is something handed over, or "traditioned." The very words are binding on the Corinthians because they did not come merely from Paul, but through Paul, through whatever community discipled him, reaching directly back to Jesus himself.

Paul resorts to this same line of argument in 1 Corinthians 15. Here the issue is right belief. "For I delivered to you as of first importance what I also received, that Christ died for our sins in accordance with the scriptures, that he was buried, that he was raised on the third day in accordance with the scriptures, and that he appeared to Cephas, then to the twelve" (vv. 3–5). The tradition here is the same gospel that we spoke of earlier, and it should be believed not because of the force of Paul's imagination, but because Paul has merely been a transmitter of what was handed to him.

When it comes to authority in the church, the job of an overseer or bishop (*episcopas*) is to pass on what he received. Bishops have no authority to invent doctrine. They are not sovereigns, but stewards. "[A bishop] must hold firm to the sure word as taught, so that he may be able to give instruction in sound doctrine and also to confute those who contradict it" (Titus 1:7, 9). Tradition in the New Testament, then, is much more than human invention. The sure word is handed over, or "traditioned." The question is, whose word, and which tradition?

Demonstrating that Jesus is the Messiah of Israel is one of the major tasks of the New Testament. The hope of the gospel rests on the idea that in Jesus the promises of God were fulfilled—promises made to Israel (2 Cor. 1:20). Obviously, many in Israel, including its high priest and the Sanhedrin, rejected any notion that Jesus was or is the Messiah. Jesus was, in their view, a blasphemer.

The church, at that time, had to defend its discontinuity with the tradition of Israel. Moreover, Christianity was changing from a movement within Judaism to one with a predominantly Gentile population. If Christianity was a faithful extension of Judaism, why did most Jews reject Christian claims? The book of Acts tackles this issue head on. Jewish persecution propels members of the church out of Jerusalem (Acts 8:1). The gospel goes to the Gentiles because, in fulfillment of the words of Isaiah, the Jews will not listen (Acts 28:25–29). The work of God in Christ and the Gentile mission are the fulfillment of the tradition because they are the whole point of God's work through Israel.

The second century brought new challenges to the church. In addition to persecution from the outside, arguments arose within the church regarding the true nature of the faith. One of the greatest challenges came from the Gnostic expression of Christianity. In Gnosticism, which means "knowledge," individuals of true understanding receive mystical knowledge of the true meaning of the cosmos. To be "saved" is to awaken from the dream of the physical world. One's eternal soul must transcend the narrow confines of the material world and reconnect to "eternal spirit." Gnostic beliefs put at risk central Christian doctrines such as the goodness of creation, the incarnation of God in Christ, and the resurrection of the body.

It may come as a surprise that these Gnostics thought themselves to be the true Christians. Yet we need only be reminded of Emerson's words: "The true Christianity—a faith like Christ's in the infinitude of man,—is lost. . . . Let me admonish you, first of all, to go alone; to refuse the good models, even those which are sacred in the imagination of men, and dare to love God without mediator or veil."[48]

The church had to defend both its distance from Judaism, in the case of the New Testament, and later its continuity with the faith of Israel in the case of Gnosticism. Irenaeus, bishop in Lyons, rose to the task. "He must define salvation in such a way that it is continuous with the physical creation and the Saviour so that he may be continuous with the God of Creation and the Old Testament."[49]

Irenaeus defined salvation as "recapitulation."[50] He built this theology on Ephesians 1:9–10. "For he has made known to us in all wisdom and insight the mystery of his will, according to his purpose which he set forth in Christ as a plan for the fullness of time, to unite all things in him, things in heaven and things on earth." Irenaeus argued that Christ "sums up" or "unites" heaven and earth, the past with the present and the future, and humanity with divinity. Christ is the thread that ties everything together. The material world is not an evil place to escape from. In Christ, the material is united in righteousness to the spiritual, and grows up into all that creation is supposed to be.

Gnostic leaders claimed to have special revelation given them directly by God. In opposition to this claim, bishops like Ignatius of Antioch argued that there was no "secret teaching" from Jesus existing outside of the community of the apostles and those they ordained. A faithful and legitimate bishop would teach only what had been handed on to him. This position developed into the doctrine of apostolic succession.

Remember, Reformers like Luther considered tradition nothing more than human invention. In response, Roman Catholics asserted that tradition was an independent source of authority entrusted by Jesus to the apostles, who subsequently handed it on to their successors, the bishops. But this position misses the point of apostolic succession. The gospel was handed from bishop to bishop openly. The connection was physical and directly involved people. There were no secret stores of information hidden from the full body of the church, accessible only to the special few. This is where the term *catholic* comes in. *Catholic* means "universal" or "according to the whole." "The whole" means what was believed, prayed, and acted upon in all of the churches, reaching back to the time of the apostles (the term is used about two generations after the apostles). The trusted interpretation did not come as a secret; it was shared by the whole. The bishop's task is not to hide and preserve, but to defend the deposit of faith for the sake of the church.

At this early point in the church's history, authority was not set firmly. Irenaeus articulated which authorities the church ought to trust. The church should trust the Scriptures of the Old Testament and those writings that are read everywhere, that is, the New Testament (the Gnostics rejected the Old Testament altogether and respected the writings of Luke and Paul only after they cut out all the Jewish parts), and the Rule of Faith, an early form of the Apostles' Creed used at baptisms. The Rule of Faith describes who Christ is, so it explains how Scripture should be read. Furthermore, the church's celebrations of baptism and Eucharist rehearse the story of all that God has done in Christ (a Gnostic would have to alter traditional language and imagery employed in baptisms and communion, because they are rife with Old Testament language).[51] Lastly, Christian behavior has a distinct character that affirms creation and the body, and demands virtues consonant with the practices handed on from the greater church reaching back to Christ himself (as we saw earlier in our interpretation of 1 Peter).

The authority on which Christianity rests is an amalgamation of all we have mentioned. All of these authorities take their cues from the central assumption of the tradition, namely, that Jesus is Lord and Savior. These various authorities all witness or testify to this one astonishing announcement.[52] Tradition, for the early church, is neither human innovation nor a separate stream of information. *Tradition* was the name given to the whole of the church's life as it works, in the Spirit of Christ, to bring everyone, everything, and every situation under the rule of Christ.[53] The tradition was not an end in and of itself. The tradition is the specific, thick life of the church. As St. Paul said to the Corinthians, "You are a letter from Christ delivered by us, written not with ink but with the Spirit of the living God, not on tablets of stone but on tablets of human hearts" (2 Cor. 3:3).[54]

Conclusion

The Transcendentalists of Concord would be very troubled with McWorld. They threw off tradition in the name of the dignity of the individual. Their diagnosis was right: tradition can be bitterly cruel; it can be a horrible shackle. Their cure, however, could not have been more wrong. One might argue that they have been misunderstood. We should not have taken their individualism without their accompanying stress upon virtue. Nevertheless, when we define ourselves only against tradition *as* tradition, we doom ourselves to narrow emotivism and the will to power.

The evidence is all around us. We should be asking questions about an idea of rights that cannot tell the difference between pornography and art, between hate speech and free speech.[55] We should be asking questions about a tradition that destroys all that came before. We should not accept the incoherence and willfulness of what Hans-Georg Gadamer calls the "one prejudice of the Enlightenment that defines its essence: the fundamental prejudice of the Enlightenment is the prejudice against prejudice itself, which denies tradition its power."[56] The ideal American, "the individual emancipated from history, happily bereft of ancestry, untouched and undefiled by the usual inheritances of family and race; an individual standing alone, self-reliant and self-propelling" ends up a frustrated parent buying a Happy Meal to placate the kids.[57]

Without the forming power of tradition, the goal of life is lost in a dark tangled wood of the self. We look into ourselves for meaning and find despair. One need only picture Edvard Munch's haunting painting *The Scream*. Without tradition, we are plastic—shaped by whatever produces the most heat.

As it turns out, tradition is something inherent to life itself. History cannot be understood without a sense of where persons fit into the whole. Science advances not in a vacuum, but upon and through accepted paradigms. Religious dialogue cannot happen when people assert that we are all really saying the same things, we just don't know it. Moral reflection is impossible apart from tradition.

The ghetto is something to be feared, but so are assimilation and secularization. Domesticated traditions are mere shadows of living ones. When Christians accept the Emersonian tradition, they become *pochos,* "neither hot nor cold" (Rev. 3:15), or "waterless springs and mists driven by a storm" (2 Peter 2:17).

Emerson gave us only two options, the free individual or the prisoner to tradition. This false choice has also been put forward by the fearful voices commenting on the horrors of September 11. All distinctions are tantamount to *jihad.* The two poles are all there is, fundamentalism or pluralism, impermeable boundaries or no boundaries. The church must live somewhere between, or transcend, the ghetto and McWorld. It must exercise discernment to steer a course between fundamentalism and syncretism. It must live somewhere on the border.

The concept of tradition is an essential navigational tool. We keep our bearings in life by telling the stories of our origins, by going back to the beginning and mining those foundational tales for today. When traditions do not grow and respond to circumstances, they become the stuff of taboo and superstition. Living traditions, Christianity included, do either change or die. If, however, they cut loose from the past to change into something utterly different, if their adherents accept another "paradigm" such as "experiential expressivism" for Christianity, they are like an uprooted tree, cut off from their life source, doomed.

Tradition should be understood as a kind of vine. As it grows, it must be looped back and tied into the primary vines. For Christians, the choice is not between Scripture and tradition or between the hoary past and the rational present. The choice is between faithful and unfaithful *traditioning*. They must continually ask themselves, Does this change bear the fruit of righteousness? Does this change honor "the commandment of God" or the "traditions of men?"[58]

Traditions must be taken on by each new generation to remain living; they must be passed on. Disciples of any tradition must truly inherit the wealth of their ancestors. They must own and invest and risk and pass on. As Goethe wrote, "What you have as heritage, take now as task; for thus you will make it your own!"[59] Irenaeus said of the faith, "We do preserve, and it always, by the Spirit of God, renews its youth."[60] Or, as Newbigin writes to a Christian audience:

> But if the parents and teachers are wise, they know that their work is not truly done until the child has reached the point where he or she can say, "Now I see for myself. Now I know the Lord Jesus Christ as my personal Lord and Savior.[61]

3

Of Hyphens
and Burned Bridges

*The Cultural Heirs
of Desi Arnaz*

Ricky Ricardo (the classic TV sitcom character from the *I Love Lucy* show) is a Cuban-American Fiddler on the Roof. He is, according to the writer-critic Gustavo Pérez Firmat, the great exemplar of what it means to "live on the hyphen." Appearing on the show with his Tropicana Night Club Band, Ricky waves his arms and pounds his conga drums with all the gusto of Tevye the Dairyman's klezmer fiddler. He does it with all the flair of one who knows himself to be founding father of a highly commercialized "Latino" culture whose progeny include Ricky Martin and Gloria Estefan. But at some level, he also knows that his band and his music have an expiration date.

At some level Ricky knows (and we the viewers know) that all of this exuberance is as much a farewell gesture to his land of origin as it is a celebration of that place. The *I Love Lucy* episode of October 22, 1951, dramatizes this well. Lucy, afraid that her young husband's affections for her are flagging, has concocted a scheme to spice things up a bit. She has just greeted Ricky decked out in a Carmen Miranda outfit (fruit hat and all) and has decked out the living room in things that she takes to be Cuban—but that look more like props out of Disney's *Three Caballeros:* sombreros, serapes, bananas, and a couple of palm trees. (Well, she got the palm trees right.) Ricky's response is not the warm, affectionate one she was hoping for. In an outburst of macho testiness, he informs her that if he had wanted things like this, he would have stayed in Havana.

What is interesting about this little outburst is what it reveals: Ricky's ultimate aim is not to keep the culture of his motherland alive, but to assimilate into the melting pot—even as he capitalizes on his "exotic" roots. To his viewing audience, he is the befuddled Cuban husband with an accent that is by turns both comical and suave. From his own perspective, he has burned his bridges and has embarked on the process of putting all of that behind him, capitalizing all the while on his heritage for the show-business success it can bring him. Like that poetic speaker in Paul Simon's song "The Coast," he seems to have thought to himself: "That's worth some money, when you think about it."[1]

Ricky Ricardo is thus annoyed at this attempt to rekindle romance with a few props from his motherland. He is here to spice up the melting pot with a few new rhythms and words, but he is not out to nurture his own piece of the cultural mosaic. He is not going to shift the magnetic pole of his life back in the direction of Cuba. He is here to teach a few mambo steps, and if he is anything like the "mambo king" Cesar Castillo in the novel *The Mambo Kings Play Songs of Love,* he will also use his accent and looks as an instrument of seduction.

It is interesting to note, even in our more self-consciously "multicultural" America, the extent to which many of the exponents of "Latino" literature and music see themselves as inhabiting an unstable, transitional zone—one whose unique, hybrid culture has an expiration date. The exuberance of the writing and the music, the crankiness at the well-meaning gestures of the Lucys of the world, both are masks concealing a sense of loss. Living on the hyphen is a bit like walking on a tightrope or fiddling on a roof; sooner or later there will be a great fall, for the dominant culture (Anglophone, consumer-oriented, secularizing) has the force of gravity on its side. There are analogies within the life of the church—as many Christians of late have come to realize. Living on the hyphen between what Martin Luther called the "Two Kingdoms" tends to stack the deck in favor of secularization, of cultural attrition.

It is common nowadays to criticize the "hyphen" as part of a "separatist" mindset. Nonetheless, the hyphen still favors ultimate assimilation at the expense of the immigrant's mother tongue. The political/cultural argument over the hyphen masks the deep-seated agreement that exists on the teleological ideal of an American monoculture; the argument is between two types of liberalism—the "fast-track" and the "slow-track" forms—over the speed with which the traditions of the Old World are to be shed.

This chapter deals with Latino writers whose roots are in the Spanish-speaking Caribbean region (Cuban-American for the most part). The first half of the chapter will focus on those writers and cultural figures who articulate this sense of living on the hyphen: Oscar Hijuelos, Gustavo Pérez Firmat (who coined the phrase), and even Gloria Estefan. The second half of the chapter will deal with those writers who attempt to transcend the hyphen and build (or rebuild) bridges back to the land of their grandparents. These include the two writers cited as the most accomplished in the field of "Latino" literature: Cristina Garcia and Julia Alvarez. Through our engagement with these five cultural figures, a couple of major points will be made:

(1) that there are striking analogies between Cuban-American culture and that of the evangelical sector of the church—given both groups' paradoxical attachments to the mindsets of "exile" (or ghettoization) and consumerism (or McWorld); (2) that one of the major ways to cultivate the space between the ghetto and McWorld is *bridge building* across spatial and temporal borders—not just pursuit of "hyphenated" identities.

Ricky Ricardo's Hyphenated Heirs: Oscar Hijuelos and Gustavo Pérez Firmat

No single event has done more to promote Desi Arnaz's mythical stature than the publication of the Pulitzer Prize–winning novel *The Mambo Kings Play Songs of Love* (1989), by the Cuban-American novelist Oscar Hijuelos. The novel revolves around the life of Cesar Castillo, the "mambo king," a fictional character who bears some interesting resemblances to the real-life Desi and is played by Armand Assante in the 1992 movie. Cesar (an impulsive, lascivious character) emigrates from Cuba to New York in the late 1940s with his brother Nestor (a more brooding, tragic, and introspective type, played by Antonio Banderas). Together they form the band The Mambo Kings and achieve ephemeral fame in the mid-1950s with a guest appearance on the *I Love Lucy* show.

The late 1940s are a time when the United States is opening its borders to workers from its neighbors to the south and is ripe for its first "Latino music" fad—for the exotic rhythms (mambo, cha-cha) and dance crazes that will follow in their wake. The youth of the postwar generation are caught up in this craze, which prefigures the Ricky Martin and Gloria Estefan craze of the 1990s. Among these youth, somewhere in the crowd must have been present another of America's great fictional icons: the young Homer Simpson, shedding his mid-American inhibitions with reckless abandon. (Fans of *The Simpsons*, take note:

dancing the mambo is one of Homer's favorite pastimes—along with eating pork rinds and playing catch.)[2]

The mambo's flash-in-the-pan cycle of commercial success parallels the meteoric and tragic fate of the two Castillo brothers. First, the melancholy-but-gifted Nestor is killed in a car accident circa 1955. Cesar, who has always lived a life of decadent excess, begins his painful descent into a life of pathos and alcoholism, and then to premature death. The novel is punctuated throughout with descriptions of Cesar's sexual exploits, which read like off-color anecdotes but grind to a slow halt as the book reaches its pathetic dénouement. In stages, Cesar also comes to take on the brooding and introspective temperament of his dead brother, as if to keep him alive.

If Cesar embodies the spirit of the mambo (frenetic, lascivious, inarticulate), then Nestor embodies that of the bolero, the Latin American "torch song" or "song of love" alluded to in the novel's title. The bolero lies at the opposite pole of Latin music in significant ways; it is mellow, sentimental, and articulate; it is what Cole Porter might have written had he been Cuban or Mexican. It is the type of song that Frank Sinatra, Ella Fitzgerald, or Harry Connick Jr. might have wanted to perform, given a command of Spanish. Nestor's one great composition is the bolero "Beautiful Maria of Soul," performed by Antonio Banderas on the movie soundtrack. It is Nestor's brooding lament over the loss of his first love, an obsessive grief that will haunt him all the way up to the fatal car crash that ends his life.

As important as these two brothers (Cesar and Nestor) are, it is, in the final analysis, the young Eugenio (the point-of-view character) who frames and filters their actions. Eugenio is Nestor's son and Cesar's nephew; one suspects he is also the author's mouthpiece. And what is most significant about Eugenio is the oblique, critical distance he takes from the exploits of his father and uncle. He seems to grieve even as he celebrates; he bids farewell even as he introduces these great exponents of the mambo and the bolero to his American audience. He glamorizes them even though he exposes the pathos and emptiness of their lives. The novel's ending leaves us with a sense that, all along, we have been present at a funeral: the funeral of a short-lived consumer craze that consumed two gifted lives. It was a craze condemned to expire in a run-down tenement in the Bronx, but to live on as a phantasmal presence (an occasional reference) in the vast ocean of the American melting pot:

> And now I'm dreaming, my uncle's heart swelling to the size of the satin heart on the I Love Lucy show, and floating free from his chest over the rooftops of LaSalle. . . . A beautiful flower-covered coffin with brass curlicue handles, and the Cardinal has just finished saying Mass and giving his blessing. . . . And when I look, there is a full-blown mambo orchestra straight out of 1952 playing a languid bolero, and yet I can hear the oceanic scratching, the way you do with old records. Then the place is very sad, as they start carrying out the coffin, and once it's outside, another satin heart escapes, rising out of the wood, and goes higher and higher, expanding as it reaches toward the sky, floating away, behind the other.[3]

Phantasmal presences. Satin balloons rising toward the sky. Such is the fate of the "mambo kings" who defined life on the hyphen.

Gustavo Pérez Firmat, professor of Spanish at Duke and author of *Life on the Hyphen: The Cuban-American Way* (1994) and a memoir titled *Next Year in Cuba* (1995), fancies himself an updated version of Ricky Ricardo. Writing from his suburban ranch-style home in the New South, and recently remarried to an American woman (his "Lucy"), he is the very profile of the exotic-yet-assimilating Cuban-American. Toward the end of his memoir, he states:

> I fancy that our rather zany lives are the stuff from which sitcoms are made, an *I Love Lucy* for the nineties. Imagine that before Lucy

married Ricky she already had grown children from a previous
marriage. Imagine that Ricky himself had been married in Cuba
and had children by his Cuban wife. . . . In the place of an apart-
ment in New York, put a suburban home in the New South. For
Ricky's nightclub, substitute Duke University. I'm Ricky Ricardo
with a Ph.D. and Mary Anne is a Lucy who would rather stay
home but can't afford to.[4]

By choosing Ricky as a model, he is reaching back to a time
(the early 1950s) before the Cuban-American experience was
defined by political exile. It is an appropriate model for one
who has left behind the insular ghetto of Miami's Little Havana
and faces the wider horizons of the U.S. melting pot, North
Carolina–style.

Pérez Firmat has good reasons to want to leave Little Havana
behind, even though he retains nostalgic ties to both it and the
vaguely remembered Cuba of his childhood. The Cuban enclave
can be a fortresslike, stifling, and intolerant place. Its ghettolike
mindset, nurtured by nostalgia and the promise of return to Cuba
and the overthrow of Fidel Castro, has proven too confining for
people of Pérez Firmat's generation. Describing a visit back to
his parents' home, he says:

> I felt hemmed in, too big for the bed and the room and the house.
> I thought of Gulliver in Lilliput. I was Gulliver in Little Havana.
> Although I clung to the exile life, it wasn't my life anymore. The
> well-being that I had felt with Mary Anne told me so. The exile
> life didn't fit my body or my soul, and I was terrified by the
> prospect of spending the next thirty years the way I had spent
> the last thirty, in a cozy, cramped, Cuban cocoon.[5]

This "cocoon" that Pérez Firmat describes bears some interesting resemblances to the evangelical/fundamentalist "withdrawal
from the world." Both the Cuban-American anti-Castro exiles
and the fundamentalist exiles from the secularizing melting pot
have sought to save their respective subcultures by withdraw-

ing into an enclave, setting up their parallel institutions, and making their language a public language within those borders. If both movements toward ghettoization had the merit of preserving certain traditions, they also disfigured their traditions in the process.[6]

Unlike evangelical scholar Mark Noll, who draws from a rich (Reformed) tradition of cultural engagement to guide him beyond the evangelical "ghetto," Pérez Firmat must go it alone, deep in the heart of the American melting pot. Pérez Firmat is an uprooted Cuban-American and a "nominal" Catholic who has opted for a more noninstitutional, self-styled form of faith that marks a drift toward secularism and cultural attrition. He fears (and he is right) that his children are destined to "melt into" the American mainstream:

> My children, who were born in this country of Cuban parents, are American through and through. They can be "saved" from their Americanness no more than my parents can be "saved" from their Cubanness. Like other second-generation immigrants, they maintain a connection to their parents' homeland, but it is a bond forged by my experiences rather than their own. For my children, Cuba is an endearing, enduring fiction. Cuba is for them as ethereal as the smoke and as persistent as the smell of their grandfather's cigars (which are not even Cuban but Dominican).[7]

He inhabits the hyphen alone. Like Desi Arnaz. Like Cesar Castillo, the mambo king. He feels powerless, in the ultimate scheme of things, to resist the American melting pot and its pact with McWorld. The hyphen does lie between the ghetto and McWorld, but it is a fraying tightrope that is bound to snap, given another generation. This feeling of inevitable attrition perhaps also explains the nearly insignificant role that religious faith plays in Pérez Firmat's memoir. His passing references to "confirmations, baptisms, etc." suggest that he is little more than a "cultural" Roman Catholic. It seems safe to say that what is happening to his children's "Cubanness" has already happened to his church affiliation: it has become a much more marginal and superficial part of his life. The ritual smoke of church incense, like the smoke of Cuban (or Dominican) cigars, does not remain around of its own accord.

Gloria Estefan: The Joys and Perils of Building Bridges in a McCarthyist Milieu

It is not surprising that Pérez Firmat should find in Cuban-born Gloria Estefan the most visible public embodiment of his life-on-the-hyphen thesis. She and her entrepreneur husband, Emilio Estefan (the major force behind the Latin Grammys), have spiced up the American melting pot and done much to spur the status of Spanish as a fashionable commercial language. But while the Estefans have done much to promote the careers of individual stars (Ricky Martin's, Marc Anthony's, Shakira's, and Gloria's own), there is little in this business that would express and sustain the life of distinctive communities. Their music is made for a Spanish-speaking "lifestyle enclave," not for the popular festivals of the U.S./Mexico borderlands, or the barrios of Old Havana. Gloria Estefan's career (which does not lack its fine moments) is in the end both formed and constricted by the ultracommercial and neo-McCarthyist milieu of cosmopolitan Miami.

At first glance, Estefan's career seems to fly in the face of the American melting pot. Is she not, after all, making music in Spanish, and does this not make her the protagonist of a vital cultural survival? Perhaps, but only in a limited sense. There are brief, shining moments in her career, like her album *Mi tierra* (1994), where she returns to Cuba's musical roots and offers some fine (if somewhat overpolished) renditions of traditional musical styles. Albums like this, though, have not enjoyed the same commercial success that her "anglophone, watered-down salsa" has had.[8] To the extent that her music is made for Latin-

American consumption, it seems best suited to the globalizing middle and upper classes, who do not feel rooted in particular regions, places, or nations. In the United States, her music seems designed for a commercial lifestyle enclave. Even her most "regional" songs have the feel of a polished marble figurine, produced for tourist consumption.

Real regional music (like the popular, plebian Mexican *música norteña*) has had a hard time gaining entrance into Emilio Estefan's musical empire. Some would even say it remains a second-class citizen; the spotlight shines on that music in Spanish that can sound most like Madonna, Top Ten, or MTV. The satirical magazine *Pocho.com* (which reads like the ethnic equivalent of evangelicalism's satirical *Wittenberg Door*) expresses this perspective in an article titled "Emilio Estefan Declares Latin Grammys an Independent Nation":

> "I banned all banda," said the new leader of the Latin Grammys. Mexican regional music, as Banda, Norteño, Rancheras and other Mexican hillbilly music is known, accounts for more than 60 percent of Latin music sales in the U.S. "I don't care how much money it makes, I put the No, in Norteño," shouted Estefan, dressed in a drab olive green outfit to his Estefanistas in a Miami plaza. Supreme Leader Estefan has allied himself to a ruling junta composed of his powerful record company friends in order to continue a proud American television tradition: Keep the Mexicans off TV. "Everybody knows the American viewing public only wants to see upper class Cubans like my wife Gloria on TV."[9]

The Latin Grammys have done well in bringing a select number of Latin American (and Latino) artists to the attention of a mainstream public. But they have little connection to regional, communal traditions. And given their commercial bent and need to attract advertisers (Budweiser, Ford, and Verizon, to name three prominent ones), they are more likely to provide us with the soundtrack for a new Spanish-language edition of McWorld—McMundo or McCondo,[10] if you will.

The problem is in the cultural/political context of Miami, which has not been hospitable terrain for that fabric of cultural practices and institutions that lie between the ghetto and McWorld. An artist like Gloria Estefan is caught between an aging ghetto of Cuban exiles (the most hard-line of which are bent on reclaiming power in Cuba and creating a McCarthyist political climate in Miami)[11] and the lure of a consumer culture that has attracted her generation and those younger. If the Cuban-American ghetto is like a house whose members are tuned in to Havana awaiting the fall of Castro ("Next Year in Havana"), the back door of this house opens onto McWorld. The capitalist consumer culture has a special backdoor entrance to this exile ghetto because of its fierce anticommunism and its entrepreneurial spirit. What is missing for the members of this exile community is a real borderlands connection to the land of its birth (impossible because of the embargo) and a strong public space that lies between the culture of exile and the culture of consumption. In the absence of these things, the culture and music of Miami are bound to be reduced to one more consumer lifestyle choice.

Evangelical Christians raised in the latter part of the twentieth century will recognize theirs as a parallel dilemma. Fundamentalism drove evangelical Protestants into a ghetto, but this separatist ghetto tuned in to the second coming of Christ ("Next Year in the New Jerusalem"), had certain affinities for capitalist consumer culture and mimicked certain aspects of it (its bland popular music, its lavish styles of consumption), and opened up a backdoor entrance to McWorld. Having attended little to the public space that lies between the ghetto and McWorld, this sector of the church in particular now finds itself in a situation in which its faith runs the risk of becoming trivialized. Its language, like the Spanish of the Latin Grammys, enters the public arena in a watered-down, marketable form.

In 1997, Estefan got in trouble with leaders of the Cuban exile community for a very modest attempt at bridge building.

She argued, in the name of free speech, that Cuban musicians (including those still in favor with the Castro regime) be allowed to perform at a music festival in Miami. This comment was part of a letter she wrote defending a Dade County advisory board member who had been fired from her job for making the same argument. Estefan followed up her letter with the comment, "Yes, I'm in favor of musicians coming here from Cuba. Why not? . . . That's freedom, the right to choose. I don't like Silvio Rodriguez, but if he wants to sing in Miami, he has the right to do so. I won't go see him. To each his own."[12] A modest defense indeed; one prefaced by a requisite denunciation of Castro, communism, and the singer-songwriter Silvio Rodriguez (who deserves to be considered Latin America's answer to Bob Dylan, and whose sin is to have retained the official favor of the Castro regime.)[13]

In a tirade that must have sounded chillingly amusing, Estefan was denounced on Miami radio as a communist. Her defenders rushed to her side, as if to shore up her tarnished image. One website devoted to her defense reads like a resume of anticommunist credentials; it quotes a number of her fierce denunciations of Castro, her defense of the embargo, and her song lyrics calling for an end to the regime.[14] Estefan's voice, in contrast to all this, is a relative call for moderation in a local power structure that too often mimics and mirrors the repressive tactics of the regime it is trying to displace. It also points to possibilities for a sustainable bilingual culture that can enrich America with its public presence.

But still, cheers for the Estefans have to be withheld. This is not out of any simple desire to be contrarian, but just because this Latino culture, filtered through the politics of Miami, is such a narrow segment of Hispanic culture. Any student of Latin America is bound to note what is omitted from, as well as what is included in, this new, urbane, cosmopolitan sound. Along with all the great Cuban musicians who have not fallen afoul of the Cuban regime, there is a glaring omission of everything that is folk and popular culture. As authentic as Gloria Estefan's boleros are, they remain in the final analysis the music of an emerging middle class (some might say "bourgeoisie"). There is little or no room, in the music empire of Gloria and Emilio Estefan, for the rich diversity of popular folklore. The rich, but less polished sounds of the Buena Vista Social Club, the samba music of Rio de Janeiro, and the music of Silvio Rodriguez himself have been made available to U.S. audiences by "alternative" and art-rock musicians like Ry Cooder and David Byrne. Estefan's music is about building international bridges to and from the Latin American middle classes, not to and from local communities with their festivals and struggles.

The Cuban-American culture of Miami has been throughout the latter part of the twentieth century a culture of hyphens and back-door connections to the consumerist melting pot. It has not attended well to festivals and pilgrimages of the kind alluded to in chapter 1, or to bridge building. The following section looks at two major authors who attempt to build bridges over and beyond this impasse but still find themselves constricted by it.

Dreaming of Bridges to Replace Hyphens: Cristina Garcia and Julia Alvarez

If Gloria Estefan is a selective bridge builder, connecting the music of Miami to the culture of the Latin American middle classes, the novelist Cristina Garcia is like the dreamer-architect, envisioning what a bridge between Miami and Havana might look like—breathing new meaning into the phrase "bridge over troubled waters." Her novels are full of characters who seek ways beyond the polarities that have divided anticommunist Miami from communist Cuba. Her novels are also full of lyrical descriptions of eccentric larger-than-life characters and skillfully rendered "magical realism" that recall the work of Isabel Allende.

Two of her novels, *Dreaming in Cuban* (1992) and *The Aguero Sisters* (1997), describe generations of families divided by personal and political passions—on both sides of the Florida Straits and both sides of the political fence. In the words of one critic, she "offers guarded hope for building bridges across ideological divides."[15]

Dreaming in Cuban's use of multiple perspectives is a bridge-building exercise in and of itself. It offers us the whole range of colliding views and the personal reasons the characters have for either loving or despising the Cuban Revolution. Pilar, a young Cuban-American who has come of age in New York, the granddaughter in this three-generation cast, is the central character, at least in our reading. Of all the characters, she seems to come closest to being the author's mouthpiece, as one who wants to build (or at least imagine or dream) a bridge back to Cuba and to establish a reconnection to her grandmother Celia, who remained behind as a faithful Castro supporter.

Pilar has her own reasons for wanting to do all of this, both personal and political. As an artist and a follower of the emerging punk-rock scene, she is tired of the Manichean "black-and-white" view of the world that she has gotten from her parents and is eager to explore the gray areas in between the hard-line stances. At a more personal level, she is alienated from her mother, Lourdes (who combines hard-line anti-Castro views with a cold, authoritarian treatment of her daughter), and hopes at some level to satisfy her "hunger of memory" and the need for a maternal nurture that was never satisfied by her own dysfunctional upbringing:

> I feel much more connected to Abuela Celia than to Mom, even though I haven't seen my grandmother in seventeen years. . . . She's left me her legacy nonetheless—a love for the sea and the smoothness of pearls, an appreciation of music and words, sympathy for the underdog, and a disregard for boundaries.[16]

The other major character in the novel is Pilar's aunt Felicia (Lourdes's sister) who has remained behind in Cuba, but whose attitude toward the revolution is more passive and ambivalent.

Where Celia seeks meaning, emotional health, and a compensation for unfulfilled longing in the ideals of the revolution, her daughter seeks similar things in the practice of Santeria (an Afro-Cuban syncretistic religion that bears a strong resemblance to voodoo). Her initiation and visits to the *babalao* (high priest of Santeria) do not deliver in the end, since she dies of the psychosomatic maladies she was trying to cure.

It takes Felicia's death, along with the death of their frail brother Javier and much pleading from Pilar, to get Lourdes back to Cuba. They arrive in 1980, during the days preceding the exodus of Cubans on the Mariel boatlift (that year's massive exodus of refugees that brought thousands to Miami). While Lourdes launches into tirades, and schemes to get her nephew Ivanito out of Cuba, Pilar spends time with her grandmother. Pilar succeeds at the personal level, in forging the bond that she always wanted, but decides that she is much too Americanized (in spite of her radical discontent with America) to spend any significant amount of time in Cuba:

> I wonder how different my life would be if I'd stayed with my grandmother. I think about how I'm probably the only ex-punk on the island, how no one else has their ears pierced in three places. It's hard to imagine existing without Lou Reed. . . . I wonder what El Lider would think of my paintings. Art, I'd tell him, is the ultimate revolution.[17]

She does not succeed as a bridge builder, or even in imagining what such a bridge might look like. But the author does manage to conjure up a vision, and it is woven into the structure of the novel itself: the multivoiced structure that gives us the whole range of colliding viewpoints. The Russian critic/philosopher

Mikhail Bakhtin would have called this technique "heteroglos-sia"—the coexistence of multiple "languages" and perspectives within a society or a novel. (His opposing term, "monoglossia," points to what we are calling McWorld and the melting pot—a homogenizing, centralizing force within the nation-state or the world at large.)[18]

The bridge that Garcia is imagining, or "dreaming," as the title of the book suggests, is a bridge wide enough to contain a heteroglossia of languages, dialects, and ideolects. It must be wide enough to contain hordes of marathon runners, each one jockeying for position in the tournament of narratives. Such a bridge still seems a long way off. It needs to be much wider than the one Gloria Estefan celebrates, or is even allowed to sing about, in the current cultural-political climate of Miami. And, of course, it also needs to be much wider than Castro's party-line rhetoric (and his crackdown on dissent) down in Havana.

If Cristina Garcia and Julia Alvarez are two of the best writers in the current field of Latino literature written in the United States,[19] then it seems a logical suggestion that the greatest novels come out of a longing (an unfulfilled and frustrated one) to build bridges. Both Alvarez and Garcia are writers who inhabit the hyphen and dream about building something more substantial and lasting, but have trouble getting a footing. Their cultural angst, the sense of urgency and tension they feel, drives them to produce the best novels in the field.

Julia Alvarez is a Dominican-American writer, who, like the Cuban-Americans we have been reading about, is a child of political exile. Her father fled the Dominican Republic with the family in 1961, after being implicated in a conspiracy against the right-wing dictator Rafael Leonidas Trujillo. His regime lies at the opposite pole from Castro's, but it is the more typical case in Latin America, and its effect on people's lives proves just as traumatic.

How the Garcia Girls Lost Their Accents (1991) is Alvarez's first novel. It covers the experience of her family's flight for their lives into exile and their four daughters' coming of age in America. In spite of the father's reformist (left-leaning) views, the family's lifestyle in the Dominican Republic was that of the Latin American elite (with a large house and a retinue of servants), and his attitudes toward his wife and daughters is authoritarian and patriarchal. The daughters thus face a loss of social status in their move to New York, as well as the tension between their nascent feminist views and their father's old-world attitudes.

Yolanda (the autobiographical character in the novel) comes of age before the 1970s, when the hyphenated consciousness started to become the vogue. Her first impulse, then, parallels that of Richard Rodriguez: to master English even at the expense of Spanish, and even to the extent of becoming an English major. Unlike with Rodriguez, though, the beginning of the novel finds her back in the Dominican Republic, trying to reestablish her roots, and perhaps even to resettle there: "Yolanda is not so sure she will be going back. But that is a secret."[20] The route of fast-track assimilation has led, for her, to a fragmented sense of self, a nervous breakdown, and two failed relationships (paralleling the author's first two failed marriages).

The novel has an unusual plot structure; it moves in reverse chronological order. This has the effect of taking us "backward" into the past, in a quest for roots, and providing us with a context in which to place the often irrational, sometimes shocking behavior of the characters. If Yolanda has problems, the behavior of her three sisters seems even more dysfunctional. Her two older sisters (Sandra and Carla) have dealt with the trauma of displacement by turning inward: to sullen introspection in Sandra's case, and to a career in psychoanalysis in Carla's. Their response is symptomatic of the therapeutic nature of modern American culture, about more of which will be said in the next chapter. The behavior of the youngest daughter, Sofia, is the most defiant and ultraindividualistic. She is the one who is most willing to shock and humiliate her father, in ways that even the American reader will find extreme.

Yolanda, in her return to the land of her birth, seems to have recognized at some level that her sisters' responses to their melting-pot experience have driven them deeper into isolation and uprootedness. So her response is to move back to where she came from, not to make her alienation even more extreme by retreating into herself and severing ties to her past.

But alas, her return to the Dominican Republic proves a bitter disappointment. Like Pilar in the Cristina Garcia novel, she fails to make the connections and build the bridges she was hoping for—and for some of the same reasons. Both of them discover that they are too "Americanized" to ever fit into the constraints of life in the Hispanic Caribbean. Pilar would miss her *Village Voice* scene and all of the bohemian artistic freedoms she enjoys there; Yolanda would miss the relative freedoms she enjoys as a woman in the United States. One of the things that her relatives make painfully clear to her is that a woman of her class is expected to restrict her movement to certain well-defined social circles and to take all the requisite care for her appearance; it will not do for her to wear the informal attire of a Peace Corps volunteer. There is a barrier between social classes that contains not just an element of cultural discomfort, but also an element of fear. There is still a rigid class system that, even in the absence of a dictatorship, can make life on the island seem like a police state. In this same first chapter, a young boy who helps Yolanda look for guavas is struck by a local guard for not knowing his place, for not keeping the social distance that hierarchies require:

> The overhead light comes on; the boy's face is working back tears. He is cradling an arm. "The guardia hit me. He said I was telling stories. No dominicana with a car would be out at this hour getting guayabas."[21]

If Yolanda's experience ends on this pessimistic note, the experience of the real-life author does not leave things there. Alvarez has learned from writers like Maxine Hong Kingston that a tradition need not be defined by the oppressive ways in which it has been experienced. Kingston's famous novel-memoir *Woman Warrior* deals with the ways women were silenced and driven to suicide in traditional Chinese culture, but it also finds the resources within that tradition to challenge those things. Kingston found within the Chinese legend of *Fa Mulan,* the "woman warrior," the inspiration to challenge the silence surrounding the death of her aunt, who was abused and driven to suicide by the townsfolk in her village on account of her out-of-wedlock child.[22]

Thanks to this insight, Alvarez went on to write what critics consider to be the two finest novels in the Latino canon: *In the Time of the Butterflies* (1994) and *In the Name of Salomé* (2000). These two novels are about the "women warriors" of the Dominican Republic's national tradition. The former is about three sisters (the Mirabal sisters) who were assassinated during the last days of the Trujillo regime (the same regime that almost took the life of Alvarez's father) and have since entered the Dominican pantheon as national martyrs. The second is about the life of Salomé Ureña de Henríquez, a Dominican poet and activist who has been unjustly overlooked in the Latin-American literary canon. Space does not permit a more detailed description of these two great novels, but suffice it to say that they help Alvarez find her most mature writing voice at the intersection of Latin-American and U.S. literature, and contribute to our notion that traditions are in their essence dynamic, not static.

In the final analysis, though, Alvarez remains a writer of the hyphen, not the bridge. She is living proof of what great literature can come out of the tension and angst-driven quest that the hyphenated condition generates. But she is not a bridge builder per se. Such a task would involve moving to the virtual/figurative borderlands of a place like Miami or New York, where a critical mass of Dominican-Americans might sustain communal practices and traditions. Instead, she has chosen to live in Vermont, a beautiful state whose village greens and farmers' markets compensate in some measure for the plazas and marketplaces that she has had to leave behind, though they can never be the same thing. And her well-researched historical novels bear the mark of an academic Latin America specialist, more than that of a communal bridge builder. In the end, her appropriation of the Dominican tradition bears the mark of a personal, vocational choice, not of communal ties.

The hyphen might well have produced some of our greatest writing, but it is still bereft of optimism when it comes to the question of maintaining that tradition that it both celebrates and bids farewell to, whose twilight it documents.

This idea of the hyphen has enormous relevance to the life of the church—above and beyond our references to the striking resemblances between the "exile" cultures of Cuban-Americans and modern dualistic evangelicals. The fact of the matter is that "living on the hyphen" has its analogue in what H. Richard Niebuhr calls the "Christ and culture in paradox" paradigm.[23] Both "hyphenated" ethnics and dualistic Christians draw a clear line of demarcation (a "hyphen," if you will) between the temporal national realm and a more "spiritual" ancestral tradition. The "spiritualized" ethnic/ecclesial culture, having lost its moorings in real places and times (plazas, village greens, ancestral homelands) is fated to become ever more ethereal and ever more absorbed into the status quo.

Gustavo Pérez Firmat depicts his "Cubanness" as an increasingly ethereal matter (like the smoke of the Dominican cigar in suburban North Carolina), disconnected from the real life of his ancestral homeland. And it comes as no surprise to us that he foresees the inevitable triumph of the status quo, the American melting pot. In similar fashion, those who advocate the "Christ and culture in paradox" (or "conversionist") stance run the ultimate risk of melting into the individualist/consumerist/nationalist ethos that has defined mainstream culture: "Frequently, this model devolves into an implicit, if not explicit, support for the *status quo,* the current shape of society."[24] The truth about "living on the hyphen" (whether one is a Cuban-American or a dualistic American Christian) is that the deck is stacked in favor of the national term (the "American" part). "Americanness" is destined to triumph in the long term—if not always in the short term.

The multiculturalist "hyphen" and the fast-track assimilation of the purer, classical liberals do not exhaust our cultural options, though. In the following chapter, we will turn to a Jewish-American writer, Chaim Potok, who managed to buck the trend of assimilation and to transcend the hyphen through an intentional community-based ethos.

4

Traditional Communities and the Church as Communion

What life have you if you have not life together?
There is no life that is not in community,
And no community not lived in praise of God.

T. S. Eliot

Underneath the questions of tradition and freedom, and all of the stories we are looking at, lies a question as old as existence: What does it mean to be human? As we have suggested, our culture assumes that to be truly human is to be "yourself," free of tradition. On top of this, the "self" we are supposed to be is self-defined over and against community, that is, against family, church, place, or ethnicity. The editors of *Habits of the Heart: Individualism and Commitment in American Life* put it best:

The American cultural traditions define personality, achievement, and the purpose of human life in ways that leave the individual suspended in glorious, but terrifying, isolation. . . . And if the entire social world is made up of individuals, each endowed with the right to be free of others' demands, it becomes hard to forge bonds of attachment to, or cooperation with, other people, since such bonds would imply obligations that necessarily impinge on one's freedom.[1]

All of this almost goes without saying. Whether we are talking about the exalted romanticism of Emerson or Whitman, hearing the Garcia girls lose their accents, watching an artist commercialize her roots and cross over into the mainstream, or watching an icon of popular culture such as Disney's *The Little Mermaid,* it seems that the underlying message is that to be human is to escape community. To be human is to "be yourself" or "follow your heart" and, in a way, to be socially disembodied.[2] Family, church, place symbolize oppression, parochialism, dogmatism, and, worst of all, "being fake." We take as self-evident truth Rousseau's opening assertion in *The Social Contract,* "Man is born free, and everywhere he is in chains."[3]

Communities, by definition, put limits on people. Because freedom—the right to be "yourself"—is defined as noninterference, communities are barriers to being truly human. Yet, in the 1960s, young, idealistic, romantic rebels who were "just being themselves" formed communes. They ached and pined to belong. To this day, young adults and teens express themselves by dressing like everyone else in their cohort. The communal and familial bonds of immigrants appeal to us as something alive, not one more product—something one could really belong to—and at the same time are the foil against which we must rebel and the prison we must escape to "be ourselves."

Richard Rodriguez personifies this ambivalence. In his early works, he is a wistful escapee of the barrio. Escaping had its pains, but it was well worth it. He has a hunger for memory, but he's not starving. In his later works, Rodriguez becomes a kind of a pilgrim. He explores his hunger by fasting from America. But all of this looking back turns out to not be about reintegrating his past into his present, but instead a way of reasserting his independence. He is what he himself chooses to be.[4]

The "discover yourself," "follow your heart" myth is alive and well. The coming-of-age-in-America story is not to take one's adult place in the community; it's to leave the community behind. "A therapeutic culture seeks to promote the efforts of the autonomous self to discover fulfillment independent of the restraints of precedent and community."[5] When the ties that bind no longer hold inherent goodness, they are enemies of the self or objects used in one's journey of self-discovery.

One sphere of life in which the therapeutic has triumphed is love and marriage. The editors of *Habits of the Heart* also state:

> A deeply ingrained individualism lies behind much contemporary understanding of love. The idea that people must take responsibility for deciding what they want and finding relationships that will meet their needs is widespread. In this sometimes somber utilitarianism, individuals may want lasting relationships, but such relationships are possible only so long as they meet the needs of the two people involved. All individuals can do is be clear about their own needs and avoid neurotic demands for such unrealizable goods as a lover who will give and ask nothing in return.
>
> Therapeutic understandings fit many aspects of traditional American individualism, particularly the assumption that social bonds can be firm only if they rest on the free, self-interested choices of individuals.[6]

In a strange twist of events, romantic love itself has been eclipsed by this new story. Romantic love founded marriage on an emotion rather than obligation and often pitted a couple against their families. But this new account is not even really romantic. It's more of an implied understanding or contract that two people can use each other to meet each individual's chosen ends. It's

OK to use someone for a night of pleasure. Moreover, instead of romance, we now have "relationships." So, when a "relationship" is over, we should not grieve or repent. We should focus on what we "learned" from the relationship.[7] People become one more product for consumption. It's ironic, but in the name of respecting human dignity by making individual choice the be-all and end-all so we will not use, or to employ Kant's term, *instrumentalize,* people, we have ended up doing that very thing!

The editors of *Habits* go on to remark that when familial ties are not inherently good, only useful to meeting the ends of self-discovery, they become very fragile.[8] Barbara Dafoe Whitehead, in *The Divorce Culture: Rethinking Our Commitments to Marriage and Family,* goes further and deeper into this subject. In short, in the divorce culture, one's obligations to oneself trump all other obligations. "According to this new conception of divorce, leaving a marriage offered opportunities to build a stronger identity and to achieve a more coherent and fully realized sense of self."[9]

> The entitlement to divorce was based on the individual entitlement to pursue inner happiness. The new ethic of divorce was morally relativistic: There could be no right or wrong reasons for divorce; there were only reasons, which it was the task of therapy to elicit and affirm.[10]

Once again, this new idea of "expressive divorce" was built on the twin foundations of the social contract and capitalism. The governing ethic is choice/noninterference and the marketplace value of utility.[11] The effect on "social capital," that is, the wreckage on children and the destabilizing of society, are irrelevant. It seems that children too are a means of self-expression. To be human is to be yourself.

In the culture wars "family" is one of the most contested institutions.[12] Family is either idealized or demonized. It is either the dream family nobody has, or the root of every ill.[13] From its beginning with Freud, the psychoanalytic tradition identified the family as the source of all pathology. To be an adult is to break away and make your own rules. Children, especially teens, are supposed to hate their parents.[14] Mary Pipher, a psychologist, discovered the positive importance of family when her training proved insufficient to help people.[15]

She discovered that individual therapy did not consider the sickness in the culture at large that batters people. The title of her book *In the Shelter of Each Other* is taken from an Irish proverb, "It is in the shelter of each other that the people live." Her notion of what family is, or should be, is akin to Robert Frost's in "The Death of the Hired Man,"

> "Home is the place where, when you have to go there,
> They have to take you in."

> "I should have called it
> Something you somehow haven't to deserve."[16]

Pipher does not sentimentalize the nuclear family. Nevertheless, she observes that families do give us a basic identity based in relationship, not consumption.[17] She asserts that to be human is to be connected. It's not, "I think, therefore I am," but as an African would say, "I am related, therefore I am."

Families can be taken as a symbol for communal identities in general, including those of place, ethnicity, nation, and church. In Augustinian terms,

> The relation of *domus* to *civitas* is not a grinding of frictional parts, for these spheres of human existence do not diverge as types or in kind; rather, aspects of the whole are borne into the parts, and the integrity and meaning of the part carries forward to become an *integral* part of the whole.[18]

It seems virtually self-evident that communal ties are coming apart at the seams, that we assume friction and not integrity. Everyone is in everyone else's way, and to top it all off, corporate culture thrives on us seeing ourselves not as members of the body of Christ, of families, or even of a particular nation. "The words 'consumer' and 'person' have become virtual synonyms."[19]

Benjamin Barber uses the term *McWorld* for all that is individualized, global, and generic. McWorld rises above prejudice and tribalism, but it also eats away at citizenship like a cancer. Barber uses the term *jihad* for all that is communal, local, and particular. Jihad's most extreme manifestation is war, but *jihad* represents so much more in Barber's work, and in Islam. Without the bonds of loyalty and obligation inherent in that which is communal, local, and particular, democracy cannot exist. Jihad and McWorld are locked in a massive struggle. They thrive off of each other even as they fight each other.[20]

In America, as a whole, we define ourselves in opposition to communal identities—and McWorld's growth depends on it. "Globalism is mandated by profit not citizenship."[21] McWorld lives on spending—spending driven by a deep psychological hunger.[22] Identity is not a gift conferred by community or by God; we create ourselves through the image we buy.[23] The terrible irony is that this free culture promotes a profound conformism of life in the subdivisions, the new tyranny of a leveled society.[24] McWorld does promise so much, but it also leaves us hungry for memory, place, tradition, and belonging.[25]

Whether in the United Kingdom, with its resurgence of Scottish and Welsh nationalism, in Catalonia, Provence, Quebec, or in the immigrant stories we are looking at here, the issue is the same. We are pulled in two directions. We long to belong, but "embeddedness means, if not exactly subjugation to an extended communal identity, membership in entities that constrain choice."[26] Those very ties that make a communal identity meaningful are the ties that keep us from being who we want to be. We are, once again, perched on the roof with the fiddler. "History has given us Jihad as a counterpoint to McWorld and made them inextricable; but individuals cannot live in both domains at once and are compelled to choose."[27]

While *jihad* is an Islamic term, it has its analog in Christianity. Bear in mind that *jihad* means, in Islam, "resistance." It connotes the struggle to faithfully practice one's faith—to be not "conformed to this world" (Rom. 12:2) or "as aliens and exiles to abstain from the passions of the flesh that wage war against your soul" (1 Peter 2:11). These passages and those who emphasize them are often accused of sectarianism or tribalism. Now, more than ever, any claim to particularity must contend with the classically liberal suspicion that it is a threat to peace and order.

In this chapter we will make three related points: (1) The church's practices (and human nature itself) are in essence communal; (2) a grasp of humanity's essential communal nature will lead Christians to the borders of this culture, but will not necessarily wall them up in a ghetto; (3) communities are inherently good, but like everything else this side of the city of God, are fallen, must be guided and limited, and are profoundly mixed, like Christ's parabolic field of wheat and tares (Matt. 13:24–30).

We turn now to the novels of the Jewish-American writer Chaim Potok. Potok's characters and settings capture the imagination. With honesty and poignancy, he takes us inside the lives of resident aliens. Potok shows us both our need for and the pain of community. He leads us on a path between ghettoization and the melting pot.

The Novels of Potok: A Path beyond *Jihad vs. McWorld*?

Most of Chaim Potok's novels are coming-of-age stories featuring teenaged Jewish intellectuals whose parents come from the old country and hold outdated, "ignorant" ideas about religion. At the same time, there is a deep respect for those old ways of being Jewish, because they kept them alive through centuries of sojourning from one land to the next—and above all, through the pogroms and eventually the Holocaust.

The Chosen, Potok's 1967 breakout best-seller, tells the story
of Reuven Malter and Danny Saunders, two Jewish boys growing up in Brooklyn in the mid-twentieth century.[28] The story,
told from the viewpoint of Reuven, opens with a softball game
between Reuven's and Danny's yeshivas (schools).

> There were fifteen of them, and they were dressed alike in white
> shirts, dark pants, white sweaters, and small black skullcaps. In
> the fashion of the very Orthodox, their hair was closely cropped,
> except to the area near their ears from which mushroomed the
> untouched hair that tumbled down into the long side curls. Some
> of them had the beginnings of beards, straggly tufts of hair that
> stood in isolated clumps on their chins, jawbones, and upper lips.
> They all wore the traditional undergarment beneath their shirts,
> and the tzitzit, the long fringes appended to the four corners of
> the garment, came out above their belts and swung against their
> pants as they walked. These were the very Orthodox, and they
> obeyed literally the Biblical commandment "And ye shall look
> upon it," which pertains to the fringes.
>
> In contrast, our team had no particular uniform, and each of
> us wore whatever he wished: dungarees, shorts, pants, polo shirts,
> sweat shirts, even undershirts. Some of us wore the garment,
> others did not. None of us wore the fringes outside his trousers.
> The only uniform that we had in common was the small, black
> skullcap which we, too, wore.[29]

Danny's ultraorthodox team came to play in order to send a
clear message: true Judaism must triumph over the backsliders,
or *apikorsim.* In a wonderful piece of dialogue, Potok captures
the kind of trash-talking that happens between base runners and
fielders. Danny says to Reuven, "I told my team we're going to
kill you *apikorsim* this afternoon."[30]

Danny's community obviously has a deep distrust of assimilation. He lives a ghetto life, and any Jew who assimilates (even
an Orthodox Jew, who is analogous to a Christian evangelical)
is an apostate, *apikoros.*[31] To be melted into the pot, even in the

slightest degree, is to break the first of the Ten Commandments: "You shall have no other gods but me."

In the fifth inning, Reuven is on the mound and Danny is at bat. Danny hammers a ball right into Reuven's face, breaking his glasses and temporarily blinding him. Later, Danny visits Reuven in the hospital to apologize, and the boys become best of friends.

As the story unfolds, each boy wrestles not only with coming of age, but with the meaning of the Holocaust and the formation of the new state of Israel. Reuven, who is certainly Orthodox, but has no expectations placed upon him to become a rabbi, decides to become one. Then there's the boy genius, Danny. Not only is he bored, he is crushed under the expectations of his community and their old-world traditions, and above all of his father. He is expected to succeed his father and become not just a rabbi, but a *zaddik*—the spiritual head and center of his Hasidic community. Danny is fascinated with Freudian psychology and wants to become a psychologist. In the end, through much pain, Danny and his father come to an understanding, and Danny goes off to Columbia University to become a psychologist.

The Chosen ends with these words:

> Danny came over to our apartment one evening in September. He was moving into a room he had rented near Columbia, he said, and he wanted to say goodbye. His beard and earlocks were gone, and his face looked pale. But there was a light in his eyes that was almost blinding.
>
> We shook hands and I watched him walk quickly away, tall, lean, bent forward with eagerness and hungry for the future, his metal-capped shoes tapping against the sidewalk. Then he turned into Lee Avenue and was gone.[32]

As we said before, Potok's stories are so appealing because they are particular. We first turned to Potok for this study because he seemed like a wonderful example of religious (Jewish) distinctiveness. To our surprise, upon revisiting them we discovered his stories share at least one thing with *Fiddler on the Roof*—they embody the liberal myth and are full of sadness and longing; Potok hungers for memory.[33]

On the face of it Potok's novels say yes to America, and the reader does not feel a great loss in seeing characters become a little less Jewish. Potok's Jewishness is to some extent domesticated by the public/private split, for the American Dream. But while it is true that in America, Jews can get out of the ghetto, assimilation is not shown by Potok as *free*. It comes with the price of leaving behind tradition, community, and faith for a new tradition, community, and faith.

And Potok pays attention to the costs in a way that few do. We could even say that his stories are not so much about saying yes to America as they are about the cost of saying yes. Danny does walk off into the sunset, but he and all those around him survived the dark night of the soul to get there. He had been promised in marriage to a girl in the community—that promise must be broken and atoned for. He had the hopes and dreams of everyone around him pinned on him—the disappointment and public humiliation must be borne. There is fear, depression, grief, rage, many shed tears, and above all, loneliness. The truth, when it comes out, is both liberating and terribly painful.

Potok is no optimist, but he is hopeful. Change is not assumed to be wonderful, and reconciliation is difficult—but worthwhile. He walks us into the middle of the tension between the individual and community, assimilation and particularity, change and tradition. Moreover, Reuven and Danny are not as assimilated as the melting pot would have it. They wear their yarmulkes in public, they keep kosher, they are immersed in the Talmud, they regularly participate in corporate and individual prayer, and they are certainly keepers of the commandments. The Gentiles in the story are not even secondary characters. Most of us wouldn't look at Reuven and Danny and see assimilated Jews. They would stick out in an airport and conjure up images of a different world and a different time. In sum, it's probably most accurate to describe Potok as saying to America, "Yes, but here's what it costs, and be careful. And here is one way to be faithful without retreating into a ghetto."

The Image of God: Being-in-Communion

We began this chapter with the question, What does it mean to be human? The Bible asserts that we were created in the image of God. So, to be human is to be the image of God . . . but what does that mean?

The answer is not as obscure a thing as many make it. One day, Jesus was asked what the most important commandment was. His reply is well known. We brought it up in chapter 2 as the essence of the Christian tradition—or argument about the good. We could say that to be truly human, "You shall love the Lord your God with all your heart, and with all your soul, and with all your mind. This is the great and first commandment. And a second is like it, You shall love your neighbor as yourself. On these two commandments depend all the law and the prophets'" (Matt. 22:37–39). From this it follows that Christians cannot accept individualism as the definition of true humanity. To be truly human is not to "be yourself"; it's not to stay out of the way of others or to live by a code of noninterference or to not hurt anyone or to be socially disembodied; it's to love—and love involves and is involved in others.

It's unbelievably easy to have unrealistic, even delusional, notions about love and community. As the early Christian rocker Larry Norman sang, "The Beatles said 'all you need is love,' and then they broke up."[34] How many Christians have bounced from congregation to congregation, or right out of the church altogether, because they were disappointed with other Christians? Love is not free; it is the most expensive of gifts—for God so loved the world that he gave his only begotten son. Much optimistic ink has been spilled in this kind of argument: "If we would just realize we're all connected, that we're a global village, and that all our actions have an effect, then we would all want to get along, we would all want to love one another." This imagined quote is no straw man.

Have you ever thought it is unfair that we, or you, have to live with the results of the fall? We have. You have sinned and will sin because of what someone else did before recorded time. That is precisely what the doctrine of original sin means: we all suffer and are even punished because of Adam's sin. We are all connected by genetics, and by the sheer years and years of sinful behavior of those who came before us. The environment or kingdom we live in is fundamentally broken. The global village will not produce the fruit of righteousness.

To be made in the image of God—a Triune God—is to be interdependent or *co-inherent* with others and the whole creation.[35] Bishop John D. Zizioulas writes in *Being as Communion:*

(a) There is no true being without communion. Nothing exists as an "individual," conceivable in itself. Communion is an ontological category.

(b) Communion which does not come from a "hypostasis," that is, a concrete and free person, and which does not lead to "hypostases," that is concrete and free persons, is not an "image" of the being of God. The person cannot exist without communion; but every form of communion which denies or suppresses the person, is inadmissible.[36]

Two comments are in order. First, to be made in the image of God is to be in relation. In Genesis, male and female complement each other; they make each other human as divine image. They are generative, that is, they are to produce children, thereby extending communion. They are also in relationship with the natural world, cultivating the earth and drawing sustenance from it, and serve as stewards of all living creatures. Second, as we observe the fallout of Adam and Eve's infamous meal, all those relationships turn sour. Adam and Eve hide their bodies from each other. They hide from God. Childbirth comes with the cost of pain. The helping, completing, one-flesh relationship becomes political—she will desire her husband in some distorted way, and he will rule over his wife (which always carries some abuse and results in some resentment). Farming will now be a struggle, and an animal is killed to cover their nakedness. When they believed the lie, they lost community and home. Like it or not, whether characterized by love, hate, or indifference, we are all involved.

C. S. Lewis dramatizes this involvement richly in *The Great Divorce*.[37] That fantastic morality play begins in hell. In hell, people, or ghosts of people, move further and further away from one another. They cannot abide others; they fear, abuse, distrust, and so on. The connections are too painful, so they flee others—and as they do so, they become more ghostly. They become infinitely smaller, becoming less human or, more accurately, disintegrating into the nothingness of chaos. Lewis obviously follows Augustine's teaching that "the loss of good has been given the name of 'evil.'"[38] The devil and his minions do not have bodies. "Evil is the unbearable lightness of nonbeing."[39] We use this language in popular parlance when we describe vice as that which makes us small and petty, and virtue as that which makes more and more of us.

We humans are involved, connected, interdependent, co-inherent, yes. But how? What kind of love is a love that makes us more human? Whose love makes more of us? Which love leads to joy and peace? The love that makes us more human is the love of the one who is fully God and fully human. Christ's love is this: "Greater love has no man than this, that a man lay down his life for his friends" (John 15:13).

If our interdependence is not pointed in the right direction, it will be hell, and lead to nonbeing, *disembodiment*. Augustine, in his magisterial work on the Trinity, explains this truth with a fascinating analogy. The analogy runs from a trinitarian doctrine of communion to a psychological point about life. The human mind exists, but only in knowing and loving. At the same time, we cannot love without knowledge, and we cannot truly know without loving. Without experience and truth, who can say they truly love a place or a food, much less another human being? Yet, it takes love to pursue knowledge. The great teachers awaken love in their students. Even when the truth is dark or difficult, it is truly known because we are driven by some kind of love.[40]

If our co-inherence is not characterized by knowledge and love, we are disintegrating. In a sense, to be made in the image of God is true love. The Greek patristic fathers developed a similar idea. Love is communion or participation in the life of another. We cannot share our lives, or share of someone else's life, if we do not know one another. So, there is no life without truth (John 11:25), and without love, we are nothing (1 Cor. 13).

Ephraim of Syria was the abbot of a monastic community in the fifth century. Dealing with the ordinary troubles of community life, he compared Christianity to a wheel. If God is the hub and we are at the circumference, the spiritual life is a journey to the center. As we move toward God, we also move toward each other. Jesus summed up the whole of the Torah by quoting Deuteronomy's dual command to love God and neighbor.

Although we often associate the famous love chapter, 1 Corinthians 13, with weddings and, of course, romance, the real love interest of that story is the church. In fact, all behavior and all personal endowments are judged by the standard of their effect on the community. In chapter 14, verse 12, St. Paul writes, "So with yourselves; since you are eager for manifestations of the Spirit, strive to excel in building up the church." The church is so communal, by nature, that Paul uses the metaphor of a body to describe it. "For just as the body is one and has many members, and all the members of the body, though many, are one body, so it is with Christ. For by one Spirit we were all baptized into one body—Jews or Greeks, slaves or free—and all were made to drink of one Spirit. . . . Now you are the body of Christ and individually members of it" (1 Cor. 12:12–13, 27).

"As a careful study of 1 Corinthians 12 shows, for St. Paul the body of Christ is literally composed of the charismata of the Spirit (charisma = membership of the body)."[41] The virtues of the Christian tradition, namely the fruit of the Spirit, do not exist in individuals, but in persons in communion. Sanctification is not the property of an individual; it is the work of the Spirit in us in communion. Over and over again, the ethical life is not about abstract rules, but about edifying the body of Christ.

Earlier, we considered how baptism and Eucharist are encapsulations of the whole Christian tradition. Here again, both sacraments can be understood only in communal terms. The quote we drew from 1 Corinthians 12:13 on baptism illustrates the point. Baptism should not be understood only in terms of washing away sin, but also as birth into the community that embodies the tradition. This point is made clearest in Ephesians. St. Paul turns the sojourner metaphor on its head in Ephesians. Usually, the metaphor is used to show that Christians are set apart from the world, such as in Philippians 3:20, "our commonwealth is in heaven," or in 1 Peter, "live as aliens." In Ephesians 2:19 the idea is that until we became part of the body of Christ, we were strangers and sojourners, but in Christ we are "fellow citizens with the saints and members of the household of God." The point at which an individual comes to have personal faith is in a sense irrelevant. The dividing wall is torn down not by our faith, but by Christ. Moreover, the whole point of salvation is to be in Christ, and Christ is in his body via the Spirit. As a wedding ceremony begins a marriage, baptism begins our life in the church. All of which is to say, you cannot be a Christian without the church.

This is why we cannot baptize ourselves! When we sink into the mires of individualism, baptism ceases to make sense. Baptism and communion are not mere ceremonies. They are enactments of the gospel; they create the church. Zizioulas writes:

The Eucharist reveals the Christ-truth as a "visitation" and as the "tabernacle" (John 1:14) of God in history and creation, so that God can be beheld in the glory of his truth and partaken of within His communion of life. The Church has therefore no other reality or experience of truth as communion so perfect as the Eucharist. Christ Himself becomes revealed as truth not in a community, but as a community. Because the Christ-truth is not only revealed but also realized, in our existence, as communion within a community, truth is not imposed upon us but springs up from our midst. Yet this truth is not the product of a sociological or group experience; it comes clearly from another world, and as such is not produced by ourselves.[42]

Returning to 1 Peter, most conversations about "the priesthood of all believers" miss the point of the passage. The issue is not who may have access to God—the ordained or all believers. The issue is that "once you were no people but now you are God's people" (1 Peter 2:5). The other metaphor employed by St. Peter is of a spiritual house into which we are built as living stones. The idea is of a mason walking through a quarry, picking out stones—especially the overlooked useless ones—and then building those stones into a temple. So while we were useless, God chose us. God did not choose us because we were special. God chose us to be his community or nation. Our sacrifices are our lives, in community, that testify to the truth that we "have been born anew to a living hope through the resurrection of Jesus Christ from the dead" (1:3). By living out this tradition, in community, we are aliens and exiles in any culture (2:11).

The Lord's Supper, or Holy Eucharist, is also known by the name Holy Communion. For ages debate has raged over just how Jesus gets into the bread and wine—or doesn't—so we can "commune" with God. The debate has swirled around 1 Corinthians 11:29: "For any one who eats and drinks without discerning the body eats and drinks judgment upon himself." It has been assumed "the body" in question is that of the risen Lord in the bread. This focus misses the point. The "body" is none other than the one Paul writes about all the time—the people. Their disregard for the body is shown by their factions, immorality, fascination with spiritual power, and general disregard for one another. As William Willimon sees it, "Paul tells them that the Lord's meal is a different kind of religious meal, even as Christianity is a different kind of religion. The sacramental reality is the act of table fellowship. *Koinonia* is the test and the result of true *eucharistia*. The 'real presence' of Christ is in the assembled worshiping community, formed by virtue of Christ's death and resurrection."[43]

As it turns out, this reading is no novelty. St. Augustine wrote of the bread used for communion, "It is your own mystery which is placed upon the Lord's table; it is your own mystery you receive."[44] Calvin recognized this truth as well when he paraphrased the Didache (9:4) for one of his prayers: "As the bread which is hallowed for the common use of us all is made from many grains so intermingled that it is impossible to distinguish them from one another, so ought we to be so united among ourselves in an indissoluble friendship, and what is more, we receive there one and the same Body of Christ so as to be made members of it."[45]

To fail to discern the body, is to *not* become a charismatic fellowship. To ignore the body or to pursue any of the vices listed in the epistles or to proclaim another gospel is to be removed from the fellowship in which the Spirit tabernacles, is to be a dead stone (1 Peter 2:5, 9–10). Fellowship is a communion of love. Christ is truth, and truth is realized not in individuals, but through the Spirit in or as church, persons in communion. St. Augustine summed it up well in an invitation to communion:

> The faithful acknowledge the body of Christ when they are not ashamed to be the body themselves. . . . That is why the apostles explain the meaning of this bread to us with the words: "We

who are many are one bread, one body"(1 Cor. 10:17). O sacrament of love! O sign of unity! . . . Whoever seeks life can find
a source of life here. Let him come forward and let himself be
incorporated, and he will be given life. Let him not shrink back
from the binding of the members to one another. . . . Let him
hold firmly to the body.[46]

We have been trying to tease tradition and community apart
to look at them both, but it's ultimately futile.[47] Vivisection
won't work, because life itself is not just a noun, but a verb.
Life is a gift. The Emersonian quest is a chimera. When we
read Richard Rodriguez, Hamlet's words about his mother
come to mind: "Methinks the lady doth protest too much."
To talk about his emancipation and autonomy, he has to tell
us about his family, and about growing up brown. Even when
we are denying our past and our people, they are with us, part
of us.[48]

Potok dramatizes this reality in a later novel, *The Book of
Lights.*[49] The protagonist is unencumbered; he is cut off from his
tradition and his people and is therefore profoundly powerless
and lonely. He becomes a person as he reengages and reconciles
with tradition and community. He does not ignore the failure
or sins of his community, nor does he try to simply turn back
the clock.

Or again, in *The Promise,*[50] the sequel to *The Chosen,* even as
Reuven incorporates new and dangerous forms of scholarship
into his study of the Talmud, he does so with a deep love for
the tradition, a profound sense of compassion for those who
cling to the old ways, all in the context of the daily/yearly
rhythm of prayer and practicing the particular virtues of
keeping Torah. Reuven and his father, a world-renowned
Talmud scholar, are talking about their new methods; Reuven
asks, "How do I convince him [Rav Kahlman, his traditional,
autocratic Talmud teacher, who is a concentration camp sur-
vivor] that the way we study Talmud is not a threat?" "But

it is a threat, Reuven. I just told you it is a threat. In the hands of those who do not love the tradition it is a danger-ous weapon."[51]

Later, Reuven is talking with Abraham Gordon, a scholar who has reinterpreted Judaism along the lines of William James. Reuven likes his questions, but dislikes his answers. They are talking about the cost and dangers of ordination, and of revising the tradition. Gordon says to Reuven, "Of course, that's the problem. . . . How can we teach others to regard the tradition critically and with love? I grew up loving it, and then learned to look at it critically. That's everyone's problem today. How to love and respect what you are being taught to dissect."[52]

Reuven is able to bring the tradition forward and stay deeply connected to his community because, even though he is critical, he is humble. He does not really dissect the tradition, but ap-proaches it as something living. So, Rav Kahlman passes Re-uven on his ordination exam, even though he detests Reuven's methods.

> "Once I had students who spoke with such love about Torah that I would hear the Song of Songs in their voices." He spoke softly, his eyes half closed. "I have not heard the Song of Songs now for—for—" He blinked. "I did not hear the Song of Songs in America until I heard your voice at the examinations. Not your words, but your voice. I did not like the words. But the voice . . ."[53]

Potok gives us characters who cross boundaries. His stories are not just Horatio Alger stories. He represents a shift from simple melting-pot ideology to something more nuanced. His characters carry an ambivalence that Christian sojourners can learn from. They are clearly Jewish first, and as the Nazis dem-onstrated all too well, being Jewish is not just an opinion, but a people. Locke would distrust them as much as he distrusted

Catholics. Jews and Catholics challenge liberalism because they are communal. In the same way that knowledge cannot be divorced from tradition, the person cannot be divorced from community. Liberalism turns Torah into a purely human invention, and sacraments into the metaphors of experiential expressivism. Liberalism dispenses with the election of Israel, and grace given through the sacraments in an institutional church.[54] Revelation cannot come to or in a particular community, because liberalism's idea of the state depends on every person being orthodox unto himself or herself.

Barber hinted at the problem liberalism has, but his proposal falls short of the goal. Barber believes that democracy needs religion, for without it we lack a stable foundation for morality (a well-known argument made by the founding fathers), and without religion we lack communal identities necessary to produce the loyalty to others necessary to sustain a republic. Problems abound with this assumption; the very idea that the sojourning communion of Christ exists for the benefit of the state or the culture is obviously idolatrous.

The related modern view is that religion is so important that it is private. Religion, any religion, is not private and does not deal with opinion, but with truth. Because religion deals with truth, it also deals with morality—and morality spills over into the principles that govern how we get along in society. Stanley Fish shows the shell game liberalism plays with religion. When religion is speech, it's free, and when it's action, it's feared and regulated.[55] Christians should have deep problems with liberalism. Religion impacts everything, from our ideas about property to sex to art to war to education and on and on. Religion cannot be private, because it deals with truth in the lives of social beings.

Our communal identities are torn apart not just by consumerism, but by liberal individualism itself. When family is not rooted in creation, but is merely a social convention, and when the church is viewed as a voluntary association, and not as the body of Christ, they both end up as one more commodity to be judged and used by that Emersonian, unencumbered, socially disembodied self.

When we try to build a city without God, when we have it our way, bracketing God out of the public sphere, confining God to the private and the voluntary, we are operating under the same (modern) ideals as the French or communist revolutions. Is this rhetoric too strong? Is liberalism peaceful, whereas all that is local and particular is violent? Consider Thomas Jefferson's startling words, "Rather than that [the French Revolution] should have failed, I would have seen half the earth desolated. Were there but an Adam and an Eve left in every country and left free, it would be better than it now is."[56] The implication is chilling: all that came before proto-liberal revolution was darkness and imprisonment. The bloody Terror was well worth the rebirth of humanity.

Generally, liberalism does not outright attack faith; it accommodates it. Fish writes:

> Accommodation is a much better strategy than outright condemnation, for it keeps the enemy in sight while depriving it of the (exclusionary) edge that makes it truly dangerous; and best of all, one who accommodates can perform this literally disarming act while proclaiming the most high-sounding pieties.[57]

When Christians operate under liberal assumptions, we have been domesticated, killed with kindness. We have become practical atheists, living so deeply in the world that we forget we are not of it.

St. Augustine's Two Cities, Communal Beings, and the Virtue of Prudence

The modern assumption is that since communities can be abusive, we should put an end to any community not of our individual choosing. Here, we are instead recommending a kind of rapprochement with traditional communities, but an open-eyed one. We are reclaiming St. Augustine's doctrine of the two cities. Augustine was no liberal. He could not separate belief from action or creed from community. In pure classical fashion, he knew most human problems had to do with communal membership.[58] If we had only one loyalty, life would be simple. If Christianity could be the soul of culture, as H. Richard Niebuhr wanted, that would be easy.[59] If the church were pure, and all other relationships were simply erased, that too would be simple.[60] The problem is, of course, that these two cities "are in this present world commingled, and as it were entangled together."[61]

The melting pot, bearing the insignia *E pluribus unum* (out of many, one), also knows most human problems are problems of communal membership. The malignant genius of liberal ideology is the subtle way it relativizes all our communal memberships save our national membership. Augustine's achievement is that he relativizes all our communal memberships to our citizenship in heaven. The kingdom of heaven is like yeast not because it is invisible, but because it is everywhere. Moreover, because he honors those other memberships as God's good creations, though marred by sin, we can work out the specific relationships through discernment and that oft-misunderstood and misused virtue, prudence.

Creation and redemption, this world and the one to come, the church and the world, the city of man and the city of God are commingled. There is no one description, however, to the entangling. It differs in each and every time, place, and culture—hence, the need for prudence. What never changes, however, is the limited nature of all "belongings."[62]

Community is relative, yes, but not without content. Community is relative to the kingdom of God. God's will is that "the human race should not merely be united in a society by natural likeness but should also be bound together by the 'bond of peace.'"[63] "Bonds of affection tied human beings from the start. Bonds of kinship and affection bound them further."[64] This is where Augustine would turn *E pluribus unum* upside down. He did not call for the destruction of divisions to create unity, nor did he cast our identities in some kind of predetermined social or racial stone. Augustine envisioned an ever expanding diversity of Adam and Eve's children held together on many levels.[65] Ultimately, the city of God will not be a simple monoculture or a multicultural salad, but a harmonious chorus.

> This heavenly city, then, while it sojourns on earth, calls citizens out of all nations, and gathers together a society of pilgrims of all languages, not scrupling about diversities in the manners, laws, and institutions whereby earthly peace is secured and maintained, recognizing that, however various these are, they all tend to one and the same end of earthly peace. It therefore is so far from rescinding and abolishing these diversities, that it even preserves and adapts them, so long only as no hindrance to the worship of the one supreme and true God is thus introduced.[66]

Conclusion

Traditional communities can be profoundly life-giving as well as abusive. Our autonomous culture can be profoundly emancipating and lonely. No-fault divorce is repulsive, but so is a society that excommunicates a woman who flees an abusive husband. The unencumbered self is abhorrent, but so is racism, that is, the attitude "you're not part of my race, which is family writ large, so you are not even human." Buffet religion is nauseating, but inquisition is terrifying. When families or nations or even the church loses the ultimate horizon, the city of God, they become fundamentally rotten. Jesus was clear that the family and the state are subsidiary to the kingdom. Even while affirming the holiness of the church, the Gospels are clear that the disciples were often the last ones "to get it," and whether we are reading about the church in Corinth or anywhere else, the kingdom of God is most likely to be found in the church, but the church is clearly not identical with the kingdom of God.

Here's a sample of what we are talking about from the New Testament. Notice the antitheses present throughout.

> Come to him, to that living stone, rejected by men but in God's sight chosen and precious: and like living stones be yourselves built into a spiritual house, to be a holy priesthood, to offer spiritual sacrifices acceptable to God through Jesus Christ. (1 Peter 2:4–5)

> For time has come for judgment to begin with the household of God. (1 Peter 4:17)

> Do you not know that you [all] are God's temple and that God's Spirit dwells in you? If any one destroys God's temple, God will destroy him. For God's temple is holy, and that temple you are. (1 Cor. 3:16–17)

> I want you to know, brethren, that our fathers were all under the cloud, and all passed through the sea, and all were baptized into Moses in the cloud and in the sea, all ate the same supernatural food and all drank the same supernatural drink. For they drank from the supernatural Rock which followed them, and the Rock was Christ. Nevertheless with most of them God was not pleased; for they were overthrown in the wilderness. (1 Cor. 10:1–5)

Each of these quotations makes it clear that the church is inherently holy. It is not a mere amalgamation of people, a voluntary society whose members happen to share the same opinions about God. At the same time, however, Scripture never identifies the church fully with the kingdom of God. Scripture is painfully honest about the sins of the church.

Even the church can (and does) abuse power. All communities, made up as they are of fallen persons, are prone to this. But this is no reason to disown them or to forget that it is our nature to be communal. It is all the more reason to learn, from Chaim Potok and St. Augustine, how to value communities without overvaluing them.

5

Galilee Meets Aztlán

*Reviving Plazas, Barrios,
and Borderlands*

egend has it that around A.D. 1168 seven tribes who lived in the region that is now the southwestern United States migrated south at the behest of their war-god to found a new empire. The place that they were to settle on was an island in the middle of a shallow lake that would contain a telltale sign: an eagle perched on a cactus with a serpent in its mouth. The city was to be named Tenochtitlán, later to be known as Mexico City. The nomadic group in question was, of course, the Aztecs, and the remote northern region from which the tribe hailed was known to them as Aztlán.

After the Spanish conquest of Tenochtitlán in 1521, some descendants of these Aztecs would return to these arid, seminomadic regions as Spanish-speaking *mestizos* (people of mixed Indian/Spanish racial heritage)—as a conquered people accompanying Spanish explorers like Coronado (1528). These regions were staked out as the northernmost frontiers of New Spain—later

125

to become the northern provinces of Mexico (in 1821) and still later to be annexed by the United States (in 1848).

In 1969, a group of young Mexican-American activists gathered in Denver and issued a manifesto called *"El plan espiritual de Aztlán"* ("The Aztlán Spiritual Manifesto"). Its purpose was to define a political movement that would be an alternative to the mainstream assimilationist politics of the previous generation. Momentous events stood in the background of this declaration: Cesar Chavez's hunger strike on behalf of the farm workers, the assassination of Martin Luther King Jr., the 1968 Democratic Convention, to name a few. The document's wording reflects the grandiose fervor and idealism of those turbulent times: "We, the Chicano inhabitants and civilizers of the northern land of Aztlán from whence came our forefathers, reclaiming the land of their birth and consecrating the determination of our people of the sun, declare that the call of our blood is our power, our responsibility and our inevitable destiny."[1]

The appeal of the Aztlán legend to those young activists is not hard to understand. The conference came, as New Mexico author Rudolfo Anaya puts it, at a pivotal moment of spiritual crisis in the life of Mexican-Americans (and of the nation as a whole). It gave them a special claim on Mexico's cultural heritage (Mexico's national culture still glories in its Aztec heritage) at the same time that it gave them a special sense of belonging to the American Southwest (named as the mythical/ancestral Chicano homeland). It defined the borderland region of the American Southwest not as a separatist Balkan-style enclave (though some members of the convention were pushing for this), but as more of a "spiritual border-traversing homeland"[2] (Anaya's description). And from this act of naming came a political and artistic renaissance to which we owe much of the cultural wealth of the Southwest—as well as the increased public participation of the Hispanic population living there.

The image of Aztlán has not lost its prominence since that historic meeting of 1969. To cite a most recent example of its relevance, one could point to the East Los Angeles rock band Los Lobos and their new album *Good Morning Aztlán* (2002). The album cover shows a rising sun and a crowing rooster drawn in the folk-art tradition. In the background, palm trees, Spanish-language signs and pastel-colored block houses stretch to the horizon—the sort of urban landscape that covers eastern and southern L.A.

The presence of the sun in the foreground is not surprising or gratuitous. For in addition to being a symbol of hope and newness, it is a prominent symbol in the Aztec-inspired imagination of Mexico and its diaspora. The sun is at the center of the Aztec calendar, and according to its mappings, at the time of the Conquest the Aztecs were living in the epoch of the "Fifth Sun" (*El Quinto Sol*). Mexico is the land of often-sweltering sunshine, and the gold of its cathedrals has a sunlike luster. It is a land of stark contrasts: of a rich cultural heritage (murals, ornate gold-plated architecture) and of destitute have-nots who will die in that same desert sun in quest of America's most menial and underpaid jobs.

Mexico's "diaspora north of the Rio Grande" has irregular sunlike contours. It is brightest, of course, along the almost 2,000-mile border; that space between the Rio Grande and the Brazos River; that region that Los Angeles and Houston preside over like skyscraper-sentinels. But this diaspora space also has its solar flares, lines of flight running up the Pacific coast to San Francisco, up the Rockies to Denver, and even up along the Old Route 66 to Chicago (birthplace of the two prominent Mexican-American writers Ana Castillo and Sandra Cisneros). Unlike the more uprooted, nomadic diasporas that were discussed in chapter 3, this diaspora is a rooted one—in contact with the sights, sounds, and smells of its land of origin. Its memories are embodied in the artistic-political heritage of murals, music, literature—and even in the architectural reminders that this land once belonged to Native American and Spanish-speaking nations. It also helps, of course, that the culture of "Old Mexico" is close at hand for most Mexican-Americans—accessible within a few road-trip hours to even the humblest of working-class families. It is unique among America's immigrant diasporas in the sense that it is concentrated along a real geographic borderland.

This chapter focuses on a group of writers who speak from the United States' southwestern borderlands region: Rudolfo Anaya, Gloria Anzaldúa, Virgilio Elizondo, and Sandra Cisneros. Through our engagement with these writers (and using the term "Aztlán" as our point of departure), we make three related points: (1) that the church shares with Mexican-American culture a sense of itself as a *rooted diaspora* and shares interest in the preservation of *plazas* (both real and figurative); (2) that the church has a special reason to embrace its newfound *borderland* status: Jesus' own *Galilean* origins; (3) that Sandra Cisneros (in her novel *Caramelo*) offers the single most comprehensive portrait of the space between the ghetto and McWorld.

The post-Constantinian church is like Aztlán in that, at its best, it is also the inhabitant of a borderland, diaspora space. And the type of diaspora space that it inhabits is not a severed, divided, or uprooted one, but one that is at heart in constant communion with its members who inhabit the other side of national borders. It is interesting to note, with all due consideration of their different orders of importance and allegiance, what these ethnic and ecclesial allegiances have in common. Both cultivate memories of particular times and places (the ancient Mediterranean or the lands that were the original territories of Mexico), and both reside at the liminal margins of mainstream (national, commercial) culture.

These parallels are not lost on Rudolfo Anaya (the New Mexico author who was present at the 1969 Denver Conference), who notes the specific parallel between the migrations of the mixed-race Mexicans (or the proto-Mexican Aztecs) and the exodus of the children of Israel.[3] His novel *Alburquerque,* which receives attention in the first part of this chapter, is a significant work because it gives dramatic embodiment to themes that writers like Cristina Garcia and Julia Alvarez raised but left undeveloped: this theme of the diaspora, and the image of the plaza as the quintessential public space. As the writer of a more historically rooted diaspora, Anaya joins his voice to those of Jewish-American writers like Chaim Potok.

The term *borderland,* which we have suggested as a first-among-equals in our fabric of notions that inhabit the space between the ghetto and McWorld, will receive special prominence in this chapter. It is a term that has received theoretical prominence within the field of cultural studies over the last decade—following the publication of Gloria Anzaldúa's pioneering collection of essays and poems titled *Borderlands/La Frontera: The New Mestiza* (1987). In this collection, she carries Anaya's concept of Aztlán to its most radical conclusions—as an agonistic site of conflict where boundaries are transgressed, violated, and trespassed. For the post-Constantinian Christian, there is much to be gained from an engagement with her work—in spite of the anti-Christian stances she sometimes takes. Like Anzaldúa, the church in the post-Constantinian era is discovering the agonistic joys of border trespassing: challenging the divides between public and private, sacred and secular, etc.

Anzaldúa's voice has been the one most heard within academic circles, but there are other borderlands voices that are just as creative and groundbreaking as hers, but whose lack of "post-modern" sensibilities (or perhaps because of their Christian tone) have not echoed as well in the halls of academia. One such voice is that of Virgilio Elizondo, theologian and former rector of the historic San Fernando Cathedral in San Antonio, Texas.

It is of great interest to Elizondo that the marginal, hybrid spaces where "ethnic" cultures thrive also seem to be the preferred site of God's self-revelation. He notes in his two major works *Galilean Journey* and *The Future Is Mestizo* that this divine self-revelation, which shines always from beyond the borders of powerful nations and empires, sheds its strongest light on the poorest and most marginal regions. We have been reminded in countless ways of how that maverick rabbi Jesus of Nazareth, who also happens to be "God from God, Light from Light," stands at such a peculiar, oblique remove from emperors, five-star generals, and corporate boardrooms. He chose as his target audience the inhabitants of a marginal region (Galilee) within a marginal province (Judaea) of the ancient Mediterranean. Galilee is like Aztlán.[4]

After looking at Anaya, Anzaldúa, and Elizondo in more detail, this chapter will conclude with the most celebrated of Mexican-American authors, Sandra Cisneros. Cisneros is a borderlands writer who recapitulates the issues raised by both Anzaldúa and Elizondo, and whose lyrical style adds depth to the whole fabric of notions that this book is about. Space does not permit a discussion of the other members of the "Chicana Renaissance" of which she is a part (a movement that includes Ana Castillo, Denise Chavez, and Pat Mora),[5] so this limited focus will have to suffice. We have found Cisneros's novel *Caramelo* (2002) to be the most ambitious (as well as the finest and most relevant) Mexican-American novel to date.

Anaya: On Aztlán, *Alburquerque*, and the Church as Plaza Preservation Society

If Julia Alvarez's work has the Latin-American plaza tucked into a footnote, Anaya's novel *Alburquerque* (1992) brings it into the foreground and, one might argue, makes it the centerpiece. This is neither Anaya's first novel nor his most widely read. (His 1972 semiautobiographical *Bless Me, Ultima* is the one for which he is most well known). *Alburquerque* is, however, his most ambitious and suggestive work—the one that best incorporates many of the issues we have been discussing.

The main plot of this novel is the quest of Abran Gonzalez, an ex-Golden Gloves champion, to find his biological father. The novel takes on much larger dimensions than those of a private quest, though, as Abran finds himself drawn into the designs of the corrupt and unscrupulous politician Frank Dominic. Dominic is a mayoral candidate who wants to transform Albuquerque into a Las Vegas–style mecca—complete with gambling casinos, a boxing arena, and high-rise developments. The two cross paths when Dominic asks Abran to fight a comeback match and help him kick off his ambitious mayoral campaign. In return for this, he promises to help Abran track down his father; Dominic just happens to have a private agent, Sonny Baca, who is up to the task.

Abran's paternal quest will lead him to Ben Chavez, a Chicano writer and Dominic's friend-turned-foe, who has composed an epic poem about Aztlán and bears a faint resemblance to the author himself.[6] Abran will also discover that his mother, Cynthia (a Georgia O'Keeffe–style artist, and daughter of a rich Anglo businessman), was forced to give him up for adoption after her ill-fated romance with Ben. His discoveries all happen in the midst of a political showdown between developers and traditional communities that echoes the plot of John Nichols's famous novel *The Milagro Beanfield War*.

The novel is full of improbable soap-opera-style plot developments and characters that verge on caricature; it might be said that it reads like a cross between the TV drama *Dallas* and John Nichols's classic novel. Nevertheless, it is a milestone because so much converges here. It offers more fertile ground for the discussion of the various issues that concern us in this book than does his earlier and more widely read *Bless Me, Ultima* (1972)—a coming-of-age novel that features the protagonist's apprenticeship in shamanism.[7]

The showdown between developers and traditional rural communities/preservationists links *Alburquerque* to *The Milagro Beanfield War*. In fact, it would not be too much of a stretch to point out the kindred spirit that exists between these two writers,

Anaya and Nichols.[8] And the theme of the plaza and its environs, whose presence is more subtle in the work of Julia Alvarez, moves to center stage here. *Alburquerque* is about the showdown between Las Vegas–style developers and traditional communities whose lives revolve around plazas and watercourses.

Neighborhoods that sustain historical buildings, local merchants, and generations of families stand to lose everything in the face of Dominic's scheme. His vision of the city's "Old Town" (also known by its Spanish appellation *"La Plaza Vieja"*) would spell its complete demise:

> Dominic tapped the steering wheel as he sat at the stop light at Rio Grande and Central. This was Old Town, La Plaza Vieja, the center of old Albuquerque. The place was an important tourist attraction with its plaza, the old San Felipe de Neri Church, shops and restaurants, and already the Old Town merchants were complaining about Dominic's plan. They claimed they would lose business if the canal system bypassed them. Hell, he would triple their business. Put one of the casinos on the plaza and bring the canal right to it.[9]

Historians of Albuquerque point out that *la Plaza Vieja* is a pale reflection of what it used to be, as much a tourist attraction as it is a historic community with an unbroken link to the past.[10] And, indeed, there is reason to lament the processes of gentrification and commercialization that have made the area (and Albuquerque as a whole) unaffordable to its historic working-class residents. Nevertheless, the narrator implies that there are worse things than this preservationist-tourist arrangement. If a developer like Dominic were to get ahold of it, the plaza could face a wholesale loss of its communal/historic character, becoming nothing more than a casino playground and theme park. Dominic's schemes make even this tourist-oriented and somewhat artificial district seem like a communal haven. For like its fellow plazas in Latin American countries, the space is still designed to function as the preeminent public space: a meeting place for diverse social groups and a venue for local vendors, merchants, etc. It is the space most resistant to the changes brought by the growth of the homogeneous consumer culture of McWorld.[11]

In an era in which the locus of hegemonic power has moved from older plazas, village greens, and town centers to the boardrooms of corporations (and the offices of their favored politicians), Albuquerque's Old Town plaza is much more than a quaint place; it is a site of resistance. The Old San Felipe de Neri Church, at the north end of this plaza, is just where the church should be—embracing its historically rooted, public (but not official or corporate) status.

The church's mission, like that of the plaza with which it has been associated in Latin cultures, is to be a civic space that is no "respecter of persons." Both are meant to welcome the participation of rich and poor, of shop owners and humble vendors. Both are unlike the shopping malls, which select their patrons on the basis of disposable income and car ownership. The church is plazalike insofar as it provides a common ground on which people of different classes, and different walks of life, can mingle.

Spaces in which the church's life meets the public eye are also plazalike spaces. The church needs spaces in which to spill out of its walled confines and practice its "liturgy after the liturgy."[12] These public spaces are figurative—if not literal—plazas. The church has a vested interest in cultivating and maintaining such spaces (which might include neighboring parks, public properties, or the sidewalks on which it holds outdoor processions).

The church is a Plaza Preservation Society.

As bad as Dominic's plans for Old Town are, they are not the most nefarious part of his scheme. The major building block of his casino-studded vision involves diverting the waters of the

Rio Grande to weave a series of Venice-style canals between the Las Vegas-style gambling venues:

> "Imagine tourists strolling through our streets in the dead of winter or during spring windstorms," Dominic smiled. "The fresh water is constant, the boats take them from casino to casino, or to the art center if that's their preference. The air is sweet, the kids are at playworld. It's all within our grasp, gentlemen.[13]

When he is reminded, after unveiling his plans, that the water rights that he needs are both the lifeblood and the possession of the Indian and Hispanic communities to the north of Albuquerque, he responds by saying that he will privatize those water rights, and he is convinced that the communities will sell them to him for a share in the profits.

Dominic presents himself, among the field of mayoral candidates, as the most "modern," the technocrat free of "ideological" encumbrances (it is unclear and irrelevant whether he is a Democrat or a Republican) and one who promises to maximize financial profits for everyone. He also is the consummate proceduralist, one who assumes that all citizens will bargain as autonomous individuals, maximizing their self-interest according to certain "neutral" rules and procedures.[14] How else can one explain the smug assurance with which he presents his scheme: "We're wrapping up negotiations right now. . . . We are promising each pueblo and each land-grant village a percentage of the casinos right off the top. They also get the first shot at jobs in the casinos."[15] Dominic's rules of the game are such that one would have to be "irrational" to turn down such a sweet deal.

Dominic's schemes bring into sharp relief the common interest that traditional ("ethnic") communities and post-Constantinian Christians have in opposing that political culture (elsewhere described under the rubrics of *proceduralism* and *utilitarian individualism*) that disallows appeals to traditional, communal allegiances and authorities as public reasons for action. Both are resistant to a political culture that pushes them to bargain as profit-seeking individuals and makes communal allegiances appear irrational or outdated. This aspect of the novel seems the most prophetic, considering the battles over water rights that have sprung up in recent years in places as distant as Cochabamba, Bolivia—pitting corporations that are pushing for the privatization of water rights against the poor citizens who have watched this most basic of commodities become unaffordable to them.[16]

Frank Dominic controlled his press conference—by defining the game as one of rational self-interest and dazzling people with his impressive PR and architectural models. But he has more trouble controlling subsequent events—both the negotiations to privatize and purchase water rights, and the boxing tournament he has set up. He had not counted on Abran's growing sympathies for the traditional communities who oppose him, nor on the scandalous public demonstration that Joe Calabasa (Abran's best friend) would carry off. Joe, a Native American Vietnam veteran who has been alienated from his hometown, is outraged by Dominic's plans and has been mobilizing his hometown against them. Shaken out of his alcoholic haze, Joe ends his series of escapades with a rampage across Albuquerque with a "magical" trickster figure who appears out of nowhere and is dressed like a 1940s zoot-suiter:

> "Come on Coyote, help me now," he prayed, and the old trick-ster appeared beside him, dressed in purple pants with a gold chain draped on one leg, a bright green velvet shirt, bright red suspenders, sunglasses, a wide-brimmed straw hat, and new In-dian tewas on his feet. He looked like a pachuco from the '40s. "Key's under the floor mat, bro," the crafty coyote spirit said. "You got no choice."[17]

This touch of "magical realism" (the seamless intrusion of legend/folklore into an otherwise realistic novel) has the same function in this novel that it has in so many Latin American ones. In works like Gabriel García Márquez's *One Hundred Years of Solitude* (1967), to cite the most prominent example, episodes like this one are the stuff of everyday life in communities that are grappling with the encroachments of the modern, mechanized, profit-making world. In Anaya's novel, a coyote spirit comes to the aid of those resisting the casino-and-canals scheme; in García Márquez's novel, epic floods afflict the modern cash-cropping banana plantations. In both cases, communities whose political interests have been deemed irrational according to the standards of a profit-seeking world make a virtue of their "foolishness" and do it with an exuberance that commands attention. It is as if, in St. Paul's language, the "foolishness" of these traditional cultures had been chosen to shame the expertise of the diagram-wielding executives.

Within the English-speaking tradition, C. S. Lewis's *That Hideous Strength*[18] (often classified in the fantasy–science fiction genre for lack of a better heading) comes closest to this combination of folklore and epic showdown. This novel has the added virtue of having intuited (long before it became obvious) the common grievances and interests of traditional communities (whether Christian, non-Christian, or some blend of both) in the face of encroaching forces such as scientific rationalism and utilitarian individualism. Those familiar with Lewis's work will recall that among other nefarious designs of a small ring of expert social-scientific planners, they plot to cut down a sacred wood and build their corporate headquarters in its place. Their plans are foiled by none other than the Anglo-Saxon magician Merlin, who (like the trickster-Coyote) returns from the pre-Christian past to do battle against antitraditional (and antiecological) developers. It is no wonder that Lewis's prophetic intuitions, as dramatized in this novel, might be seen as having more relevance to our time than do his rational apologetics.[19]

Anaya's novel combines the showdown between developers and preservationists with the sort of dramatic, soap-opera-type relationships that make this book read like a made-for-TV movie. The characters might seem at times improbable and caricaturesque, but the social battles they represent are nonetheless real. Anaya's earnest idealism is a welcome counterpoint to the cynical stance of the uprooted diaspora. Though his style will be surpassed by that of more recent Chicana writers like Sandra Cisneros, his seminal influence and vision will not.

The rural Hispanic and Native American communities fighting for their water rights, as well as the inhabitants of La Plaza Vieja, are inhabiting that borderless borderland referred to as "Aztlán." This homeland is not so much a separatist territorial unit (like francophone Quebec), nor is it the uprooted diaspora space discussed in chapter 3. It is a "rooted diaspora space"—tied to the landscape and cultural space of the Southwest but not a pure ethnic enclave. It is a better description than what we have seen thus far of the kind of space the church inhabits: a space that honors a particular geographic region and a particular time (the ancient Mediterranean; the Roman province of Judaea) without claiming any geographical or political borders as its territorial boundaries. Those who fear that stressing of particular identities and rootedness in certain landscapes should remember that, at their best, the identities of church and ethnic communities do not have a "balkanizing" territorial spirit. The communities of Aztlán in Anaya's novels are like the townsfolk of *The Milagro Beanfield War,* struggling to preserve traditional lifeways; they are completely unlike the partisans of violent *jihad,* who seek to create a pure ethnic enclave with well-patrolled boundaries.

Anaya, in short, gives us a borderland with boundaries that are more like semipermeable membranes than walls, protecting the organism of a particular culture, but not walling it off from the "outside world." Behind these membranes (which mark the frontier between Mexico and the United States, between Aztlán and other ethnic cultures) lie old town plazas, and communities who fight for their water rights and remember their ancestors.

Gloria Anzaldúa's Borderlands: Agonism and Symbolism

The prominence of the term *borderlands* within academic and culture-studies circles owes much, as suggested before, to Gloria Anzaldúa's collection of essays and poems titled *Borderlands/La Frontera: The New Mestiza* (1987). Her vision radicalizes Anaya's in at least a couple of ways. For her, borders are not porous barriers, but a symbol for all the boundaries and divisions between and within people. Borders are also a site of conflict, often painful and agonistic.

Anzaldúa speaks of the geographical border between Mexico and the United States in stark terms and images. She reminds us that borders can be painful reminders of exclusion (from the wealth of wealthier neighbors, from the people and places left behind) as well as protective cocoons: "1950 mile-long open wound / dividing a pueblo, a culture /. . . This is my home / this thin edge of barbwire."[20] But she does not just speak of national borders. She writes also of the borders between genders and races, between dreaming and waking states, between the secular and the sacred. And she speaks of the creative inspiration that comes of trespassing all of these borders:

> Living in a state of psychic unrest, in a Borderland, is what makes poets write and artists create. It is like a cactus needle embedded in the flesh. I get deep down into where it's rooted in my skin and pluck away at it, playing it like a musical instrument.[21]

The paradoxical fact about living in the borderlands (symbolic, geographic, or both) is that the inhabitant is always crossing and trespassing them. Inhabitants of cities like El Paso and Tijuana live with the presence of borders as a permanent, visible feature of their lives, but no less visible is the blurring, crossing, and traversing of those same lines. By expanding the concept beyond its geographical referent, Anzaldúa has opened up space for dialogue with the post-Constantinian Christian who lives on the symbolic borderlands between the secular and the sacred—and between the private and the public. Christian and immigrant writers like Anzaldúa know that some of their most creative work and thought is the hybrid product of pushing and trespassing these boundaries.[22]

The process of hybridization can be agonistic, agonizing, exhilarating, or all of the above. It can be a cactus thorn, barbed wire, or a moment of transcendence. But regardless of how it is felt, it marks a creative frontier; the word *frontera* means both "border" and "frontier" in Spanish. Inhabiting the borderlands means inhabiting a space where ghettoized cultures are called to break out of their "cocoon" and risk engagement with the culture at large. It is also the place where that same culture at large—founded as it is on the principles of liberal individualism—is called to break out of its own cocoon and embrace a postliberal stance that is more hospitable to people's communal traditions and authorities.

In spite of what Anzaldúa offers, her work is bound to be double-edged and controversial within ecclesial circles—not least because of its rejection of the historic Christian faith in favor of a full-fledged shamanistic belief system. As if to lend fuel to the suspicion that Latin-American culture has "idols" lurking behind its "saints," she seeks out the pre-Hispanic deities and dispenses with the saints altogether.[23] Behind Mary, for example, she finds the Aztec goddesses Tonantzin (an earth-mother figure) and Coatlicue (a more ambivalent, death-and-life-giving goddess who wears a skirt of serpents): "In the U.S. Southwest, Mexico, Central and South America, the indio, and the mestizo continue to worship the old spirit entities (including Guadalupe) in their supernatural power, under the guise of Christian saints."[24]

Transgressing the borders between dreaming and waking states, Anzaldúa takes us on a descent into the world of Jungian archetypes and finds Guadalupe/Coatlicue there:

Coatlicue is one of the powerful images, or "archetypes," that inhabits, or passes through, my psyche. For me, la Coatlicue is the consuming eternal whirlwind, the symbol of the underground aspects of the psyche. Coatlicue is the Mountain, the earth mother who conceived all celestial beings out of her cavernous womb. Goddess of birth and death, Coatlicue gives and takes away life; she is the incarnation of cosmic processes.[25]

The postliberal Christian, who is more interested in the wisdom of Karl Barth than of Carl Jung, takes a much different path at this point. Instead of descending into the realm of the archetypal, he or she transgresses the borders of Enlightenment rationalism by stepping into the narrative universe of Israel and the church—and the God who is borne witness to in that narrative. And the church, as we have noted, does not lack theologians who have engaged in just this sort of fertile boundary-trespassing. The trespasser most relevant at this juncture is Virgilio Elizondo.

Virgilio Elizondo's Galilean Borderlands

Because of her neo-paganism, Anzaldúa overlooks many of the parallels between her prophetic portrait of Mexican-American culture and the counterhegemonic teachings of Jesus of Nazareth, the Galilean prophet who hailed from the despised borderlands of Judaea and the Roman Empire. But this fact has not been overlooked by Virgilio Elizondo. In *Galilean Journey: The Mexican-American Promise* (1983), published four years before Anzaldúa's collection, he develops the theological implications of the borderlands idea in a way that is fresh, visionary, and all but overlooked within academic circles.[26]

Elizondo makes much of the fact that Jesus was a Galilean Jew—that he spent most of his public life in a region that was considered marginal, "backward" and "impure" by the standards of those who occupied the centers of power in Jerusalem and

Rome. Galilee's more culturally hybrid and less scrupulous ways were held in contempt by the more "pure-minded" national religious elites in Jerusalem—who used their official favor with the Roman Empire to lord it over the commoners:

> The Jews were scorned by the Gentiles, and the Galilean Jews were regarded with patronizing contempt by the "pure-minded" Jews of Jerusalem. The natural mestizaje of Galilee was a sign of impurity and a cause for rejection. The Pharisees looked down upon the "people of the land" because they were ignorant of the law. The Sadducees looked down upon them because they were somewhat lax in matters of religious attendance and familiarity with the rules of temple worship.[27]

It is not hard to see where Elizondo is going with this. The Mexican-American (and by extension all others who inhabit the marginal borderlands of U.S. culture) are analogous to the Galileans. The power of Rome, of course, is analogous to that of Washington, D.C., capital of the world's sole superpower. And the power of Jerusalem is analogous to that of the capitals of nations like Mexico, El Salvador, and the Dominican Republic—whose elites have often profited from their special relationship with Washington (or Moscow in years past) and have tended to look down on their diasporas as culturally inferior populations.[28]

Elizondo, like Anzaldúa, finds in the borderlands a "site of multiple rejection"—a status that is marginal to both the Latin-American and the U.S. centers of power. At this point, though, their paths diverge in an interesting and significant way. Where Anzaldúa calls for a defiant affirmation of difference for its own sake ("Being lesbian and raised Catholic, . . . I made the choice to be queer"),[29] Elizondo draws on the resources of the Christian tradition to affirm difference within the context of the universal fatherhood of God. We are equal as human beings because we have a common standing before God (and are called by the

Galilean Jesus to address him in the intimate, familial language of parenthood). And we affirm our differences in the context of this equal standing—and not as part of a raw quest for power and self-assertion:

> In this intimacy with God, Jesus also reveals a new anthropology: dignity, confidence, security, docility, and self-respect based on a freely chosen dependence on the one absolute: God.[30]

It is perhaps because of this Christian anthropology and its empowering resources that Elizondo looks at the borderlands more in terms of their possibilities than their pain. Capitalizing on the "frontier" image contained within the Spanish word *frontera,* he states: "It is consistently in the frontier regions of human belonging that God begins the new creation. Established centers seek stability. It is 'frontier types' who will be the trailblazers of the new societies."[31]

Because of this basic disposition, he is in more of a position than Anzaldúa to capitalize on the image of the fiesta, of the possibilities contained within the festive nature of Latin American culture. In addition to being the means through which identities are kept alive and vibrant, the fiesta is, for Elizondo, a forward-looking, eschatological event; this is even more true of the Christian festival than the national-ethnic one. The poor and marginal are able to affirm the full stature of their being and anticipate the eschatological communion of the saints. Echoing Octavio Paz's writings on the fiesta within a more theological framework, he states:

> It is likewise there [in the Eucharist] that the despised can ignore the labels that proclaim them to be inferior and rise to the full stature of their being. It is in the truly Christian fiesta—the agape—that all experience themselves for what they truly are: children of the same father without need for distinctions or explanations.[32]

The Eucharist is fiesta-like because (in keeping with the ethos of the plaza) it is embracing of all social types and is no respecter of persons.

This festive tone marks the most important difference between Elizondo's and Anzaldúa's work, and it illustrates Elizondo's point that there must be a joyous spirit to temper the prophetic denunciations: "The prophetic without the festive turns into cynicism and bitterness."[33] Anzaldúa's work is prophetic without being festive. It stands as an act of wounded defiance, as a crossroads bridge in a war zone: "the battleground / where enemies are kin to each other; . . . you are wounded, lost in action / dead, fighting back."[34]

The bridge that Elizondo builds is not without its agonistic elements, but the resources of the Christian tradition allow him to be more hopeful, to replace raw self-assertion with confident dialogue: "As mestizos of the borderland between Anglo America and Latin America, Mexican-Americans can be instrumental in bringing greater appreciation and unity between the people of the two Americas."[35]

Elizondo takes up the images of the festival and the bridge in the same way that Anaya takes up the images of the plaza and the diaspora. He is the best example we have so far of one who has reflected on ecclesiological and ethnic-cultural issues in conjunction. In so doing he has cast a bright light on the space that exists between the ghetto and McWorld.

Sandra Cisneros: Of Reclaimed Barrios, Pilgrims, and Prodigal Daughters

Anzaldúa and Elizondo have both, in varying degrees, influenced the novels and poems of the most well-known and celebrated of Mexican-American writers, Sandra Cisneros.

She is part of the recent "Chicana Renaissance" (a term used to describe the commercial and critical success of a number of Mexican-American women writers, including Ana Castillo, Denise Chavez, and Pat Mora). All of them can be seen as developing the themes and images that we have been setting forth, and a full treatment of the subject would require a whole book in its own right. Here we will focus on Sandra Cisneros, because of her undeniable status as the most well-known among this group—and for the ambitious scope of her recent novel *Caramelo,* which we will propose as the best Mexican-American work of fiction thus far.

The House on Mango Street (1984) is the novel by which she is still perhaps best known. Like Anaya's *Bless Me, Ultima* and Julia Alvarez's *How the Garcia Girls Lost Their Accents,* it is a semiautobiographical coming-of-age narrative. Like Anaya's and Alvarez's works, it is an important-but-not-great work that reads like a series of lyrical, loosely connected vignettes depicting a young female writer's coming of age in one of Chicago's Latino neighborhoods.

The neighborhood that surrounds the narrator's childhood home is anything but idyllic; it is a barrio in the worst and most commonplace sense of the term: a slum to be gotten out of, a place that is dehumanizing for men but even more so for women—given that poverty is compounded by the fear of abuse, rape, and confinement. She knows that in order to be a writer, she will need a "room of her own," somewhere far from this place: "Only a house quiet as snow, a space for myself to go, clean as paper before the poem."[36]

A quick glance at the fate of all the women of the "Mango Street" area suffices to explain why the narrator, Esperanza Cordero (the word *esperanza* means "hope," and the word *cordero* means "lamb"), must leave. One of her best friends, for example, has left an abusive father only to be under the thumb of an abusive husband who does not let her talk on the telephone or even look out the window. Esperanza remembers the inarticulate sense of outrage and the loss of innocence she felt after seeing this same friend coerced into kissing a number of boys in an abandoned lot referred to as "The Monkey Garden":

> And I don't know why but I had to run away. I had to hide myself at the other end of the garden, in the jungle part, under a tree that wouldn't mind if I lay down and cried a long time. I closed my eyes like tight stars so that I wouldn't, but I did.[37]

What is most interesting about this novel, though, is Esperanza's ultimate resolve to return and remain part of the barrio. She goes against the grain of Linda Chavez's "Out of the Barrio" assimilationist imperative. "They will not know that I have gone away to come back. For the ones I left behind. For the ones who cannot get out,"[38] the narrator thinks to herself toward the end of the book. It is as if her situation were the direct inverse of Richard Rodriguez's. Where Rodriguez in *Hunger of Memory* set out to make a clean break with his Sacramento Spanish-speaking milieu in spite of all the good that was there, Esperanza retains her ties to Mango Street in spite of all the trauma and oppression that she sees there.

Esperanza, like Cisneros herself, understands that the places where we spend our formative years are a more inextricable part of us than the myth of the melting pot would have us believe. (And, as we have argued, even Rodriguez comes to a partial recognition of this.) Cisneros speaks of having found her voice as a writer when she came to the realization that the landscape and problems of the barrio where she grew up—and not the more "generic" locations of Anglo writers of her generation—were to be her basic source of inspiration.[39]

Coupled with this realization that the barrio—for better or for worse—would always be a part of her and an inextricable part of her voice as a writer, is the hope (*esperanza*) that the decaying barrio can be a revitalized one. Both of these notions work their way into the resolve of Esperanza (the author's alter ego, without much doubt) to return. In real life, Cisneros returned to work in inner-city neighborhoods, teaching high-school dropouts, etc. In 1984, the same year *The House on Mango Street* was published, she moved to the revitalized barrio of San Antonio, Texas—a region that also comprises the real, geographical borderlands and has been her home base since.

Cisneros moved to San Antonio in 1984 and went on to publish *My Wicked, Wicked Ways* (1987) and *Woman Hollering Creek* (1991). The latter are works that register the presence of the borderlands region and, in particular, of the taboo-breaking vision of Gloria Anzaldúa. Published the same year as Anzaldúa's *Borderlands/La Frontera*, the collection of poems titled *My Wicked, Wicked Ways* takes as its centerpiece the deliberate transgression of sexual/gender boundaries. From the controversial cover (where she poses in a suggestive vampire outfit) to the defiant feminist-outlaw persona she adopts ("By all accounts I am a danger to society. / I'm Pancha Villa"[40]), it is clear what she is going for: a street-smart feminism built to weather the adversities of the barrio she has not left behind.

If her writing career had ended on this Anne Rice–meets–Madonna note, we might have yielded to Ilan Stavans's assessment of Cisneros (an uncharitable one) as "foulmouthed and lightweight."[41] But to do so even then would have meant ignoring the genuine, lyrical depth of her style and failing to come to terms with a difficult but important question that she poses: How can a writer (or any woman) reclaim her ethnic heritage when this often implies reconciliation with authorities that place unjust demands and restrictions on women's lives? An honest engagement with this question, as well as the full blossoming of her lyrical powers, is present in her novel *Caramelo*.

Cisneros comes into her own as a writer with *Caramelo* (2002), producing what comes closest to being the masterpiece of Chicano/Chicana literature. The novel deserves to be read for both its wide-ranging breadth of subject matter and its lyrical style, which is at its peak. The reader will encounter woven into its storyline the whole fabric of images that describe the space between the ghetto and McWorld: There are pilgrimages and fiestas; there are bridges and diasporas searching for roots; there is a grappling with traditions and communal authorities; there are plazas and border-crossings. Because of its epic breadth and lyrical depth, it provides us with one of the best windows on the collection of themes that has concerned us.

Studs Terkel places the novel in the John Steinbeck tradition, praising it as "a salsified variant on the Joad family's odyssey, zigzagging from Chicago to Mexico City and back."[42] This is accurate as a brief synopsis, provided one does not fail to mention the notion of pilgrimage—even spiritual pilgrimage—that so pervades the novel. As Terkel suggests, this sprawling, 439-page book is structured around three road trips to Mexico as remembered by the narrator, Celaya ("Lala") Reyes. The three deaths in the novel, two of which occur between the road trips, provide occasion for soul-searching (or ancestor-searching) reflection. The first trip, the most colorful and tragicomic, is an ill-fated caravan involving Lala's aunts, uncles, and cousins on a trip to visit her grandparents. The trip is a disaster because of a complex web of cultural, generational, and marital conflicts that become clearer as the novel progresses. The second trip's mission, following her grandfather's death, is to bring her grandmother back up to the United States. And the third trip, following this same grandmother's death, begins as Lala's rebellious-adolescent attempt to elope, but ends up being a spiritual pilgrimage in which she comes to see her familial authorities and her familial faith in a new light.

In the course of the novel, Lala's grandmother, Soledad, develops in the reader's perception from being the authoritarian "Awful Grandmother" (as her Americanized grandchildren refer to her) to being Lala's revered ancestor and spiritual companion. And the grandmother's devout faith grows from being the stuff of authoritarian nuns to being the focal point of Lala's spiritual pilgrimage at the climax of the novel. This climax occurs as Lala, the prodigal daughter who tried to elope, now finds herself all alone in the big, overwhelming metropolis of Mexico City and stumbles on the December 12 festival in honor of the Virgin of Guadalupe. The experience turns out to be a conversion, a mystical epiphany, and a pilgrimage all rolled into one:

> Poor Virgen de Guadalupe. Hundreds of people ride the moving conveyor belt of humanity. The most wretched of the earth, and me among them, wearing my grandmother's rebozo knotted on my head like a pirate, like someone from the cast of *Hair*. . . .
>
> I look up and La Virgen looks down at me, and, honest to God, this sounds like a lie but it's true. The universe a Cloth, and all humanity interwoven. Each and every person connected to me, and me connected to them, like the strands of a rebozo. Pull one string and the whole thing comes undone. Each person who comes into my life affecting the pattern, and me affecting theirs.
>
> I walk back to the hotel. I walk past pilgrims who have walked here all the way from their villages, past dancers performing with rattles on their ankles and great plumed headdresses, past vendors hawking candles and night-light Lupes . . .[43]

To Cisneros's credit, the novel moves beyond the one-dimensional stereotypes of familial authorities, tradition, and faith that have plagued much immigrant assimilationist literature. It also illustrates how one cannot recover one's heritage without becoming reconciled, in some large measure, with the communal authorities (and even, in some cases, the religious authorities) who are the custodians of that ethnic heritage.

Behind the mystical moment that Celaya the narrator describes, there is an act of reconciliation—above all with the figure of Soledad, the grandmother. This is interesting, because the Virgin is often thought to represent an alternative to the patriarchal culture of the Roman Catholic Church. Here, however, the Virgin is not so much a quasi-goddess figure as she is a symbol of the matriarchal power with which Celaya is coming to terms.

The familial authorities that immigrant writers feel pressure to reject are often as matriarchal or maternal as they are paternal. Mexican culture may be patriarchal in the sense that male children are granted a wider range of privileges and opportunities in the public arena (to hold political office, etc., plus the unspoken freedom to have extramarital affairs and to roam the streets without fear), but they are matriarchal in the sense that mothers and grandmothers—at least in much literature and many films—are the chief enforcers of rules that constrict their daughters' lives. It is no surprise, then, that when Celaya is attempting to elope and gives up the process in desperation, the ghost of her recently deceased grandmother is there to induce both comfort and all manner of guilt. Her indulgent father, whom she calls in desperation, is quicker to forgive and offer unconditional acceptance to this prodigal daughter:

> Always remember, Lala, the family comes first–la familia. Your friends aren't going to be there when you're in trouble. Your friends don't think of you first. Only your family is going to love you when you're in trouble, mija.
>   Who are you going to call? La familia, Lala, remember. The twinkling lights strung outside the balcony are lit. In that carnival of darkness and light, I fumble for the phone and hear my voice ask for a long distance line, please, por cobrar.
> —Do you accept?
> —Yes, Yes! I hear father's voice say desperately.—Lala!
>   Lalita? Mija, where are you, mi vida?
>   My mouth opens as wide as a fatal wound, and I hear myself howl,—Papa, I want to come home![44]

How do Lala's father, Inocencio, and her grandmother Soledad come to be honored like this in a genre of coming-of-age immigrant literature whose traditional imperative has been to make a break with parents and grandparents? How does Soledad come to be an honored matriarch, after her initial entrance onstage as the "Awful Grandmother": over-indulgent with her son Inocencio, but spiteful toward her daughter-in-law and overly critical of her "Americanized" grandchildren? The answer must lie, at least in part, in Celaya's need to understand these two people who have played such a formative role in her life—and in that context to understand herself.

There is much to understand about Soledad, and the narrator devotes a large section of the novel to doing this. She was abandoned to some relatives in Mexico City just before the outbreak of the Mexican Revolution (1910–1920). As a girl, she learned the beautiful craft of candy-colored-shawl making—and the one surviving sample of her craft (the *rebozo de caramelo* that gives the novel its title) is the object that will forge the symbolic bond between her and Lala, her Chicago-born granddaughter. She was married "above her station" to a man who exercised his culturally accepted infidelity. She compensated for her solitude and isolation (the name *Soledad* means "solitude") by clinging to her son Inocencio with all of the indulgence, affection, and tenderness that her marriage must have lacked.

The grandmother, Soledad, and the father, Inocencio, are honored for their craftsmanship (she for her shawl making; he for his vocation as an upholsterer, a craft that he refuses to compromise in favor of tackier, more lucrative work). But they are honored above all because Lala realizes she cannot attain any form of self-knowledge apart from them. Her admission of this, which comes as she is describing Inocencio's declining health and his death at the end of the novel, flies in the face of the modern individualist notion of the autonomous self defined in isolation or abstraction from others (earlier she had discovered in her prodigal-daughter-turned-pilgrim flight that this is a dead-end road):

> It hits me at once, the terrible truth of it. I am the Awful Grandmother. For love of Father, I'd kill anyone who came near him to

hurt him or make him sad. I've turned into her. And I see inside her heart, the Grandmother, who had been betrayed so many times she only loves her son. He loves her. And I love him. I have to find room inside my heart for her as well, because she holds him inside her heart like when she held him inside her womb, like the clapper inside a bell. One can't be reached without the other. Him inside her, me inside him, like Chinese boxes, like Russian dolls, like an ocean full of waves, like the braided threads of a rebozo.[45]

Nor can Lala reconcile with her grandmother without coming to terms, at least at some level, with her grandmother's faith—represented in the figure of the Virgin of Guadalupe at Mexico City's basilica. Celaya's rapprochement with the church corresponds to the author's own sense of surprise at finding herself working side by side with, and writing the foreword for the most recent work of, none other than Virgilio Elizondo, a bishop of the Roman Catholic Church, which she had scorned for so long: "So far had I removed myself from my Catholic upbringing that it hadn't occurred to me that my story of searching for a voice in American letters could also be the story of someone searching for his voice within the Catholic church, of finding strength from 'otherness,' and this otherness giving direction to one's work."[46] Cisneros, as a borderlands writer, has moved from the defiant posture of Anzaldúa to the more Galilean posture of Elizondo. And her rapprochement with this most traditional and communal of authority figures is part and parcel of her return to the borderlands, her decision to nurture the space between the ghetto and McWorld, the space that she calls "otherness."

The Reyes clan is the perfect embodiment of Elizondo's Galilean, plebian borderlands. *Caramelo* bridges the landscapes of Mexico and the United States in the same way that *The Grapes of Wrath* created a narrative bridge between Oklahoma and California. Both sagas involve cramped, uncomfortable road trips along vast stretches of Old Route 66. These road trips are a blue-collar counterpoint to the flights of the middle and upper classes from Latin American cities to condominiums in Miami.

The Reyeses' saga is played out not to the soundtrack of the Latin Grammys, but to a music that is more local, regional, and plebian. Lala recounts seeing the world through the windows of unair-conditioned clunkers and being tuned in to the sights, smells, and sounds of popular plazas and street vendors. Her description of crossing the bridge over the Rio Grande at Laredo is one of the most lyrical and evocative ever written on the subject—certain to evoke the delight of recognition in those of us (like Mark, who grew up as a missionaries' kid in Mexico) familiar with the terrain:

> Churches the color of flan. Vendors selling slices of jicama with chile, lime juice and salt. Balloon vendors. The vendor of flags. The corn-on-the-cob vendor. The pork rind vendor. The fried banana vendor. The pancake vendor. The vendor of strawberries in cream. . . . The smell of diesel exhaust, the smell of somebody roasting coffee, the smell of hot corn tortillas, along with the pat-pat of the women's hands making them, the sting of roasting chiles in your throat and eyes. Sometimes a smell in the morning, very cool and clean that makes you sad. And a night smell when the stars open white and soft like fresh bolillo bread.
>
> Every year I cross the border, it's the same—my mind forgets. But my body always remembers.[47]

To be part of a bridge-building and bridge-spanning ethnic tradition is, above all, to be connected to sights and sounds like this. "The body remembers," Celaya states, speaking of those elements of popular culture that are contained within borders but also spill across those same borders. It is a remembrance that is more physical and local than abstract and official. It has little to do with government offices or bureaucratic documents, and much to do with food, drink, and street vendors—and the fabric of her grandmother's shawl. It is as if these things were the sacrament of Celaya's ethnic culture, reactivating its life in the most tangible way—like the bread and wine of the Christian Eucharist that connects our bodies, not just our minds, to a communal, border-traversing narrative.

The Reyeses' saga, as we read of it, involves all of our senses, and it is permeated above all by the fabric of the shawl, whose presence is almost tactile. The image of the shawl permeates this novel like a background canvas, and the scenes that are played out on it are scenes that fade into one another in shifts as subtle as the colors of a spectrum; scenes involving bridges, plazas, festivals, and communal authorities.

What lies between the ghetto and McWorld is contained within the fabric of Cisneros's *rebozo de caramelo.*

6

Of Fiestas
and Eucharistic Animals

*Autocracies, Democracies, and the
Need for Communal Authorities*

> *The social gospel . . . is the religious reaction to the historic
> advent of democracy; the worst thing that could happen to God
> would be to remain an autocrat while the world is moving to
> democracy. . . . God must join the social movement.*[1]
>
> Walter Rauschenbusch, 1917

*M*odernity is one long, protracted argument about authority.
*When we speak about tradition, the common assumption is
that traditions inhibit free thought. When we think about
community, the assumption is that it constricts us from being ourselves.
All truth claims—such as those about what it means to be human—are,
in this view, thinly veiled attempts to grab power.*[2] There is only one
way anything happens in this world: through dominating force.[3]

Since God is the ultimate authority, all claims about God are regarded as claims for power by whoever is making the claim. There is only one way to protect human rights: by leveling or democratizing all social relations. Even though we can't always articulate the rationale for them, we know our rights.[4]

Obviously, traditions have experts and exemplars, and communities have boundaries and gatekeepers. Tradition and community assume some form of hierarchal structure. On a practical level, everyone who attempts some form of rapprochement with traditional communities has to deal with the matriarch or patriarch, whether a grandparent, parent, or priest. Are our only options autocracy or absolute democracy?

Diagnosis: An Authority Problem

At what was Theron's first chapel at Oral Roberts University, Oral himself made it abundantly clear to Theron and the whole student body that attendance at ORU was a privilege, not a right. ORU was not a democracy. This felt tyrannical to Theron. He had come to ORU full of hope and expectation, and he left "Honor Code Chapel" confused and angry. He muttered to himself, "I came halfway across the country, and I'm paying all this money to be told I cannot question?" Theron felt violated and deceived. The whole thing felt very un-American, and it was.

During his years there, ORU was featured in the *Tulsa World,* the local paper, now and then. The oil bust had been unkind to the school's endowment, and the school was broke. Rumors circulated that the place might close because it could not pay its creditors. Worried, anxious students broke the first commandment: do not question the administration. Once again, in chapel, the student body was given a sound scolding for trusting "the secular media—a tool of the devil," and its questions were regarded as a serious threat to the administration (read: thou shalt not question Oral or Richard, for to do so is to "touch

God's anointed"—as in, Pharaoh should not have made Sarah part of his harem and David would not harm Saul because they are God's anointed).

Besides Oral's infamous "give me 12 million or God will call me home," the late 1980s also hosted the downfalls of Jim Bakker and Jimmy Swaggart. All these ministries were autocracies, led by secretive, unaccountable men. If they were associated with a particular institution, such as the Assemblies of God, they had so much power, and such a following, that censure was irrelevant. Also, since there was no tradition for passing on authority in their ministry, they, like most megaministries, were and are family dynasties, that is, autocracies.

Theron started attending an Episcopal church in 1987, during his junior year. He was a theology major and a resident advisor—a symbol of all that ORU was about, a "whole man." But he was in trouble theologically. Although he was much more ignorant than he realized, the ignorance of the preachers and teachers in the charismatic churches was downright offensive. They were always coming up with new theories, new gimmicks, new movements. Their theories lacked any sense of history or intellectual depth—and they asked for unquestioning obedience. His theology classes, though, were a bright spot that opened up a whole new world to him—not just the classic doubt that so many go through in college. He was introduced to the Christian intellectual tradition—Basil, Irenaeus, Augustine, Luther, Calvin.

Then there was that saint from Assisi, Francis. What a contrast and a challenge the *poverello* provided! The very architecture of ORU symbolizes its odd love/hate relationship with modernity. The futuristic buildings, with their golden facades, are an odd kind of gilded McWorld ghetto. Imagine twenty- to thirty-year-old, crumbling buildings, evocative of *The Jetsons,* and totally lacking any Christian symbolism—no crosses, no saints, only pictures of the first family. In the midst of all that theological chaff, St. Francis gave the lie to the Pentecostal assertion that there was no true church between the time of the apostles and the Azusa Street revivals.

So when a young man on his floor invited Theron to his Episcopal parish, he went. A Pentecostal must be rather desperate to attend a mainline/offline church—one of those churches thought to be the home of the frozen chosen, of unbelief and dead ritualism.

In the preaching, liturgy, and community life of that particular parish, Church of the Holy Spirit, he experienced two things. One: the ancient, universal, basic Christian faith. He didn't have to worry about what hare-brained theory he would be asked to assent to in a "repeat after me" prayer. He could go to church and hear the catholic faith. Two: it wasn't about him or the preacher. The liturgy of the church was bigger than any one person. The community of faith was bigger than any one person. Individuals were not the focus—God was. When God is the focus, lo and behold, there is room to be truly present.

Theron came into the Episcopal Church believing that Episcopalians believed what the *Book of Common Prayer* said, including the Thirty-nine Articles of Religion. He believed that Episcopalians believed the authorities they put themselves under were Scripture, tradition, and reason.

Then he encountered the rest of the Episcopal Church in seminary. The church was in the throes of the Righter trial. Bishop Righter of New Jersey had ordained a practicing homosexual—that is, a homosexual who had a life partner. He was accused of having broken the doctrine and discipline of the Episcopal Church. A campus-wide forum was held, and all the usual things that happen at forums happened. One of the speakers was a Washington, D.C., attorney who was a chancellor (lawyer) for the whole Episcopal Church. He argued that the charges against Bishop Righter would be thrown out.

This chancellor gave a bit of history. Back in the 1960s, heresy charges had been formally brought against a certain Bishop Pike. Pike had written that the old doctrines of the church were just that, old and outdated. So, a commission had been put together under Bishop Baines to examine the charges and the very idea of orthodoxy and heresy. The commission had reported that in this modern era it is no longer possible to call an opinion or perspective on faith heresy, because we all have different perspectives on what truth is. Pike had not been tried; so, naturally, the charges against Righter would be thrown out (and they were).

Theron was bewildered. He had come to the Episcopal Church because it represented the best of the Christian tradition, a reformed Catholicism, only to discover that those authorities that make it what it is (Scripture, tradition, and reason) were being trumped by something new and amorphous—individual perspective and personal experience. God had indeed joined the social movement of democracy.

In this brief biography, we see autocracy and democracy-run-amok in full flower. In this Emersonian world, bishops (i.e., overseers) are a logical impossibility. An *episcopas* is an authoritative embodiment of a tradition[5] (and it is really a simple equation: no authority + no tradition + no community = no *episcopas*). While the "rooted" Christians of mainline denominations subject God to a democratic vote, the rootless Christians of nondenominationalism fall into the other, antidemocratic side of modernity: autocracy. This calls for a closer look at the question of authority in our (post)modern world.

Down with the King

We must look back four hundred years. The Protestant Reformation was a battle not just over particular doctrines, but over authority. Luther invoked the principal of *Sola Scriptura*—Scripture alone—to dethrone hierarchal and traditional church structures. Protestants believed truth could be mined directly from the Bible—no other authorities being needed or valid.

Soon thereafter, the new ideas of the Enlightenment cast doubt on Scripture's ability to reveal; that is to say, Scripture's unique authority was called into question. The miraculous was deemed superstitious. What good was to be known could be known by any individual. We see a great example of this faith in reason in one of Thomas Jefferson's personal letters:

> Shake off all the fears and servile prejudices, under which weak minds are servilely crouched. Fix reason firmly in her seat, and call to her tribunal every fact, every opinion. . . . You must lay aside all prejudice on both sides, and neither believe nor reject anything, because of any other persons, or description of persons have rejected or believed it. Your own reason is the only oracle given you by heaven.[6]

In other words, anyone who trusts any authority—traditions, Scriptures, bishops—is a fool. Such a person has been hoodwinked; he or she is an irrational fundamentalist.

Truth, at this point, was detached completely from tradition and community. Truth resides in the individual, so the individual takes on a kind of ultimacy. Robert Kraynak argues that Immanuel Kant, more than any other thinker, determined the way people think about human dignity, rights, and politics. Kraynak summarizes Kant's definition of what it means to be created in the image of God:

> Kant offered the most explicit formulation of the ethical principles of human dignity that now shape Christian politics—namely the infinite and absolute worth of every human being, the unconditional duty to treat everyone as an end not merely as a means (in Kant's language as a "person" rather than as a "thing"), and the moral imperative to respect the rights of persons in a liberal democratic order.[7]

Since human beings have inherent dignity, they have inviolable rights, and are, regardless of their faith or their behavior, children of God. The defining factor of humanness is freedom, the right to fashion the world as we see fit.[8] The new doctrine makes liberal democracy a logical necessity. Christianity is equated with protecting people's rights as autonomous, self-defining individuals.

Kant's idealism meets utopian socialism in Walter Rauschenbusch. Since the old expressions for God are really props for autocratic power, we should throw them overboard. God is not transcendent; God is considered to be in us all (echoing Emerson). We do not need to have our sins atoned; rather, we need to maximize our self-development. The root of sin is oppressive, constrictive social structures.

> The kingdom of God . . . tends to a social order which will best guarantee to all personalities their freest and highest development. . . . The reign of love tends toward the progressive unity of mankind, but with the maintenance of individual liberty and the opportunity of nations to work out their own national ideals. . . . It is the supreme end of God and the purpose for which the Church exists.[9]

As the story is normally told, liberal democracy evolved over the centuries from the "Christian" idea of human dignity.[10] Buoyed by this common thread of human worth that is in both traditions, Christians during the Enlightenment/Constantinian era could believe that the most significant things God does are not in and through the church, but in and through the culture at large, and especially through the state.[11] The church, in short, could be led to accept a rival eschatology. Some bishops and historians, following in the footsteps of Eusebius, could see empires and states as anointed by God to bring about the triumph of Christianity. Their ideas would differ little from the ideas of those of old who had regarded Constantinople as the Virgin's city, and the emperor was, at the least, closer to God than everyone else—maybe even a kind of younger brother to Christ the Ruler.

American history famously equates the promised land of
Scripture with the New World. Providence ordained that God
build a city on a hill, and America would be that city.[12] Bumper-
sticker theologians illustrate the point with their JerUSAlem
insignias. H. Richard Niebuhr's *Christ and Culture* is the last,
best example of this kind of thinking. As Niebuhr argues per-
suasively, the church's job is to change culture from within (his
famous Christ transforming culture), and it is in culture that
God is working. In time this (dominant) culture came to have
such significance in our imaginations, and individualism came
to be so self-evident, that many Christians came to equate free
choice with what or who "God" is. Like William James said,
democracy is its own kind of religion.[13]

One powerful example of what equating Christianity with
democratic individualism can do is seen in attitudes toward
evangelism. Where the kingdom of God is reduced to democracy, evangelism is perceived as a form of cultural imperialism
(as it certainly is oftentimes). So, in the Episcopal Church, for
example, foreign missionaries are basically a thing of the past. The
thirty or so missionaries who are supported through the church's
national office (a tiny fraction of the number that once was), are
more like Peace Corps volunteers. Domestically, the Episcopal
Church recently set out to find a way to grow numerically. The
project was at first spearheaded by evangelicals and church growth
advocates. It has, however, been taken over by identity-politics
ideologues, that is, we must have representation from groups *x*,
y, and *z*. Evangelism is not about conversion; it's about creating
a kind of multiethnic, multi-sexually-oriented society.

Rampant individualism and thoroughgoing secularization are
the full flowering of a process we now recognize well. We have
presented these movements as part and parcel of our cultural
heritage, as the fruit of the Enlightenment Project. But they are
also as old as Genesis. First, people lack faith in the goodness
of God, that is, we distrust God's authority. Second, with God
out of the picture, as St. Augustine shows in great detail in *City*

of God, we humans try to fashion a city of our own making that reaches into the heavens. Like those ancients of Babel, we try to make our own heaven on earth.

In contrast to the autonomous individual (who has a knee-jerk suspicion of all authorities), we begin here with the notion of the human being as a "eucharistic animal" for whom "to think is to thank." Using this notion of the human being as a point of departure, we will make three related points: (1) the church should recover an understanding of the sacraments (and even the reading and interpretation of Scripture) as a kind of festival; (2) festivals (whether eucharistic or ethnic) require communal authorities; (3) authority is measured by its conformation to the image of God in Christ.

Eucharistic Animals vs. Autonomous Individuals

Adam and Eve had everything they needed for meaningful, holy lives. Rather than enjoying all they had, they became fixated on the one thing that was off limits. Through the serpent's lies, Eve came to doubt God's goodness. She doubted that God had been truthful. She ceased to trust God's authority. God was keeping something back from them, something they deserved.

The image painted in Genesis of Eden is not of a vacation, but of a vocation. Adam and Eve work. Adam names the animals. They are to reproduce. As beings in God's image, they fashion and make. Here is the crux of the matter. The proper response to this marvelous gift of a place in which to thrive, work, and love is to give thanks. We are *eucharistic* animals.[14]

Barth said it well, *Charis* always demands the answer of *eucharista* (i.e., grace always demands the answer of gratitude). Grace and gratitude belong together like heaven and earth. Grace evokes gratitude like the voice of an echo. Gratitude follows grace as thunder follows lightning.[15] To thank is precisely what the Kantian, unencumbered self must not do. As Robert

Heinlein's pragmatic anarchist hero Jubal Hershaw said, "nine-tenths of gratitude is resentment." Gadamer's proverb "To think is to thank" is anathema to Emerson's self-reliant man and Nietzsche's *ubermensch* alike.[16] If to be human is infinite possibility, ever transcending biology, history, family, whatever, then indeed to thank is to look back at Sodom like Lot's wife.

For us in this culture, self-reliance, autonomy, independence, are virtues. A common interpretation of "the fall" is that it was a necessary part of growing up. Adam and Eve were children who had to individuate by disobeying the authority figure. In our culture, obedience is a virtue in children and dogs, not in adults.[17] To even try to say, "I must obey to be true to myself" is ridiculous.[18]

Because we were raised on the social contract in this liberal tradition, the idea of obedience makes us nervous. It certainly made Theron nervous at his first Honor Code Chapel at ORU. In one way, Oral was telling the truth. The university bearing his name *is* his. However, ensuing events showed his hand as an autocrat who should not be trusted. Christians are called to obedience not in general, but in specifics: "obedience requires that we believe the one we obey is worthy of our obedience; we cannot be said to obey someone unless we believe he or she is rightfully an authority. . . . The one who obeys must ask himself if the one he obeys is worthy of his obedience."[19]

Our first parents should have trusted God because of God's character. It was a matter of faith, because Eve really did not know what would happen if she disobeyed. She trusted the serpent rather than God, even though God made them, provided for them, set them up with good work, and gave them space to work things out on their own. The God of the Bible is a Creator who speaks and "things" come to be, and a friend who shares a walk in the cool of the evening. Especially in Christ, we encounter a Lord and an obedient Son. Maturity is not had by disobeying God; it is had by thanking God as living sacrifices.

All this may make the whole process sound quite rational. The "choice" that Eve, then Adam made has a rational quality to it, but it has much more to do with trust in God's character. While they did have reasons to trust, the outcome was still unknown. It's not that faith is irrational, but that there's more to it than a sound intellectual base.[20] To obey is to trust an authority even when we cannot be sure of the outcome, and even if we are sure what we are asked to do is going to hurt. So, Shadrach, Meshach, and Abednego answered Nebuchadnezzar's threats,

> We have no need to answer you in this matter. If it be so, our God whom we serve is able to deliver us from the burning fiery furnace; and he will deliver us out of your hand, O king. But if not, be it known to you, O king, that we will not serve your gods or worship the golden image which you have set up. (Dan. 3:16–18)

Dinner for One: From Fiesta to Private Rite

In many ways, the eucharistic fiesta[21] is a crossroads at which tradition, community, and authority meet.[22] In the Old World of Europe, citizenship in the nation and citizenship in the church were one and the same. That is what Christendom is, or was. In Christendom, baptism was a familial rite of passage, and communion was a public birthright. The Puritans came to Massachusetts not to end Christendom, but to "get it right." Part of that corrective process would be that only the regenerate elect could partake of communion. One was to prove one's salvation by telling the story of how one repented and came to know God's saving grace.

This process worked well enough until umpteen immigrants arrived who could not (or would not) give their testimony. Church attendance plummeted. So, a compromise was reached, the so-called Half-Way Covenant. Children of members could be baptized, but until they gave their testimony, they could not vote or partake of communion. After a century of following this pattern, the Puritans began practicing "open" communion. Any Christian, whether able to produce a testimony or not, was welcome at the Lord's Supper.

Emerson was born into a Puritan family, the son and grandson of ministers. He renounced his pulpit at Second Church of Boston (Unitarian) in 1829 over the issue of administering the Lord's Supper. His objections follow the contours of our three categories. First, tradition: Emerson held that truth is not mediated through tradition. He abhorred the very idea that revelation came through forms, texts, or hierarchies. He argued that Jesus never intended to "establish an institution for perpetual observance." The Lord's Supper was, in Emerson's view, a kind of trope for the infinitude not just of Jesus, but of everyone. Submitting to a tradition is antithetical to self-deification.

Second, community: Emerson was a romantic. He trusted that when people followed their hearts, they would choose virtue and would contribute to the common good. He himself was a beloved father, the first citizen of Concord, a man of great virtue. His faith was in innate goodness, which was hampered by institutions, obligations, and heredity. Truth was revealed in our poetic imagination, not in relationship. Emerson wrote in his journal,

> It is when a man does not listen to himself but to others, that he is depraved and misled. The great men of the world, the teachers of the race, moralists, Socrates, Bacon, Newton, Butler, and the like, were those who did not take their opinions on trust, but explored themselves and that is the way ethics and religion were got out.[23]

Church was a good place for individuals to hear sermons, that is, to think and reason for themselves; it was not a community in and through which the Spirit works.

Third, authority: Emerson certainly believed in "God." His God, however, was fully immanent in the reasoning, expressive individual. In a sense, Emerson's real issue with tradition and community was authority, that is, their authoritative claim on his life. While arguing for his faith in himself, and in all "men," he trusted nothing outside of his own thoughts and feelings. Lundin summarizes:

> [Emerson] was ready to devote himself to the gospel of America as the kingdom of God. And he was eager to proclaim that the imagination had replaced the cross as the central symbol of spiritual experience. . . . In making the ordinance of the Lord's Supper the issue over which he broke with the pastorate and the Christian tradition, Emerson rejected all efforts aimed at sustaining the particularity and exclusivity of the gospel, and he made Christ, the romantic self, and America indistinguishable from one another.[24]

Emerson simply bypassed the whole problem of who could attend the Lord's Supper. Where Puritans continued to argue over who could partake, trying to discern who was a true member of the community, Emerson made the whole conversation irrelevant. America was the kingdom, and by virtue of our innate dignity, we could transcend ourselves and actualize God in us. All this is encapsulated in his disdain for gratitude. Lundin reports:

> On June 20, 1831, he wrote that it is not wise to belong to any religious party, for "as fast as we use our own eyes, we quit these parties." In late July he complained, "suicidal is this distrust of reason; this fear to think; this doctrine that 'tis pious to believe on others' words, impious to trust entirely to yourself." He concluded this entry with a note of sarcastic resignation: "To think is to receive."[25]

The issues Emerson struggled through are very much alive and well. Episcopalians and Methodists are arguing about communion even now. Historically, any confirmed Episcopalian was welcome at communion. With the recovery of baptism as the sacrament of full inclusion in Christ's body, any baptized Christian was welcome to commune, regardless of age, or of what Church baptized him or her. In either case, there were no official criteria in terms of one's "regeneration" or how one believed Christ is present in the sacrament. This is what Episcopalians meant when they said communion was open.

In recent years, however, in the practice of many congregations all boundaries have been eradicated. All persons, baptized or not, are now invited to the Eucharist. The gospel means inclusion; that is, it's thoroughly egalitarian and democratic. Where Tertullian said, "Christians are not born, they are baptized," the creed of this new wave of transcendentalists is quite amorphous—whatever works for you, all paths lead to the same god. Like Emerson, dignity is not a gift bestowed and lived up to with thanks; it's an innate right. It sounds so kind, so fair, so American. Yet, it's emotivism in the flesh. Emotivism has become the pseudo-intellectual basis for right and rights. Lundin draws this insight from W. H. Auden's play *The Sea and the Mirror:* When people "cannot abide authority external to the self, individuals inevitably choose to make either the body or the mind their lord and guide. Either way, however, they eventually arrive at a state in which they have become the only subjects in the world and are alienated from nature and humanity."[26] By leveling all authorities, all traditions, all individuals, we do not create a more just, sanctified world. We play right into the hands of McWorld.[27] With Emerson, we see a missed historic opportunity to make the Eucharist a public, non-Constantinian event.

The Eucharist is a type of fiesta, remembering not just Christ's last night with his disciples, but celebrating the whole story of God's gracious fellowship with humanity, as it was, is, and is to come. Its Old Testament antecedents range from Passover and the Feast of Unleavened Bread (Exod. 13), to the great covenant-sealing ceremony on Mount Sinai (Exod. 24), to the bringing of the first fruits (Deut. 26), to King David's great feast where he passed his anointing on to his son Solomon (1 Chron. 29).

Certainly the Lord's last night with his disciples was filled with grief, but the church's celebration of the Eucharist reaches back in the New Testament to the miraculous feedings in which Jesus took, blessed, broke, and gave (Matt. 14), and forward to a resurrection appearance at Emmaus with Cleopas and his friend, where, once again, in the moment of taking bread, blessing, and giving, they recognized the risen Lord (Luke 24). Also, through the gift of the Holy Spirit, Eucharist is a hope-filled foretaste of the great wedding of the Lamb and his bride, the church (Rev. 21). All of these moments, both in the Old Testament and the New, and those known to us as hope, are communal events in which the church celebrates and enters into the very heart of God's self-giving love.

This is true not just because it is meant to be a public and nonhegemonic event; it is also festival-like in the sense that Hans Georg Gadamer uses the term. It is a dramatic act whose nature is repetition-with-a-difference:

> From its inception—whether instituted in a single act or in-troduced gradually—the nature of a festival is to be celebrated regularly. Thus its own original essence is always to be something different (even when it is celebrated in exactly the same way).[28]

Every time the Eucharist is celebrated, it is at once a unique event and an identically reenacted one. And as a dramatic event, it is draped in a festival-like mantle that, according to Gadamer, covers even the act of interpretation itself. (Interpretation is, after all, just such a repetition-with-a-difference). In the church's life, the mantle covers sermons, as well as all reading and discussion of Scripture. There is ample warrant, following Gadamer, to re-gard most of what the church does in its worship and common life as being "festive."

And these eucharistic/interpretive festivals require their own types of authorities.

Equality Does Not Equal Justice; or Why Fiestas Require Communal Authorities

In chapter 5 we considered Rudolfo Anaya's novel *Alburqu-erque*. The novel, as we suggested, stands in stark contrast to assimilationist dramas like *Fiddler on the Roof.* Where *Fiddler* mournfully celebrates the destruction of tradition, Anaya brings the citizens of McWorld back into living traditional communities. Abran's mother, Cynthia, was deeply interested in the very soul of Mexican-American culture. So, in order to see and feel who these people truly were, she went to their fiestas. In her journal, Cynthia tells a graphic story about one particular fiesta, an autumn harvest festival in a rural river valley.

All the generations were represented, and food was everywhere, "steaming plates of eggs, bacon, potatoes, chile stew, hot tortillas, and coffee."[29] It was time to slaughter a couple of pigs for roasting; that was the young men's job. They had all been drinking, but were eager to prove their machismo. One man in particular, Marcos, a lawyer with a white wife who lived in the city, was to do the killing. He returned to the country for the sake of his parents and grandparents and for the fiestas. His older aunts teased him because he had forgotten the old ways.

The old men stood aside, warming themselves in the morning sun, watching. They had handed on the killing to their grandsons years ago. Marcos was drunk and angry. He did not know what he was doing. He couldn't control the pig, and he was going to use a rifle to kill it. The children were there too, playing tag, nursing, and watching. "Here was the link between past and future generations, this is how the young would learn the old ways."

Everything went wrong. Marcos fired a grazing shot off the pig, then another, but it was still alive, kicking and bleeding. Someone tried to give him a knife to finish it off, but he wouldn't take it. He vomited. Another man pounced on the pig and knifed it, but it still kicked and bled. It was a horrible, frightening thing. The children were terrified.

The old men shook their heads, the children hid, and the young men cursed each other. Marcos blamed the others for not holding the pig right. Waving the rifle around, he demanded the other pig be brought out. Voices raised until grandpa, the family patriarch, said, "No!" Grandpa insulted the young men—they couldn't even kill a pig. They were angry, but they still respected him. They made light of it; it was no big deal. Grandpa insisted, "It is a big deal. It has to be done right." They tried to get grandpa to take a drink, to back off. "I don't drink with boys," he said.

Marcos got angry, "If you're such a man, why don't you do it? Grandpa likes to talk, but he's too old to cut the mustard." Grandpa took the challenge. His friends quietly led the pig out and encircled it. With a small sledgehammer to the head, then a knife to the heart, it was done quickly, quietly, reverently.

"The compadres smiled and remembered all the years of their lives when they had done this. It was a ceremony, the taking of the animal's life to provide meat for the family. The young men needed to be reminded that it was not sport, it was a tradition as old as the first Hispanos who settled along the river.

"This is how we have lived along the river, the viejos said. We have raised generations on this earth along the Rio Grande, and we have done it with pride and honor. Each new generation must accept the custom and likewise pass it on."

The young men honored their grandfather. Every bit of the pig would be eaten or used. And the old men "had done their duty, they had shown the young people the right way to perform the ceremony."

The story is rather graphic. It is not romantic in the sense of idealizing a people. It is ironic that people who are entertained by murder and mayhem cannot stomach the killing of a pig. The story sums up so much of what we are trying to say. The setting is a fiesta: a gathering where soul happens, where all that makes individuals a people, is gathered together, lifted up, and passed on.

Tradition: a whole way of life is celebrated, and even created in the celebration. The heroes of the story, the elders, are not drugstore cowboys. They have not bought an image. They have lived a life of hard work, and that is the root of their virtue. That life is one of honor: it knows everything comes with a cost. They do not have to invent themselves, because they are connected to the past and to the earth itself. Everything is scripted: certain foods must be served, and the pig must be killed and eaten a certain way. The fiesta is a kind of pilgrimage, a journey to the edge, where the gringo ways are left behind and Mexicanos are born. This tradition is alive, and it gives life to those who share in it.

Community: that lifeway is not so much an idea as it is a sensibility which can be known only when people are together. All the generations are present, and all have a part to play. The hierarchy of the generations is life-giving. Family is not an institution stopping anyone from being "themselves." It is that home you don't have to deserve. This community holds no hegemonic power over society. It lives on the borders, away from the centers of power, and reminds us that plenty of "real things" happen outside of the capitals of the earth. It is a place of belonging—the kind of belonging that motivates people to care for children and respect elders.

Authority: the whole of this lifeway coalesces in the matriarch and patriarch. They are the heart and soul of the tradition and the community. There is neither autocracy nor modern democracy here. The authorities bring the gift of life to the generations as they incarnate the traditions. If the patriarch had not stepped in, if the hierarchal structure had not been honored, the family would have simply disintegrated. These elders do not hold total power over the family, but by tending the environment, they guide the direction of the event and see that everyone is included.

We have no interest in giving ultimate authority to anyone. We do not deny that hierarchy always comes with a measure of abuse. We are saying, however, that a way of life that assumes that all hierarchy is inherently evil destroys the communities and truncates the connections to the past that we need for our basic sanity.

Let us move from a rural valley in New Mexico to suburban western New York. This anecdote illustrates an immensely practical outcome of the Emersonian view of things.

Theron grew up in a village where it seemed most people went to church. The great divide in the culture wasn't so much between believers and unbelievers, but between Roman Catholics and Protestants. There were of course many people who didn't belong to a church, but that didn't seem to change the basic assumptions. The little village bore out what survey after survey has shown. Most Americans do not think of themselves as religious, but the vast majority believe in God.

One evening in high school, Theron was at a gathering in the home of a classmate named Roger. They had been in kindergarten together, so while they were not best of friends, they knew each other pretty well. Roger's parents' home was filled with all kinds of religious paraphernalia. All the pieces were very tasteful, very "arty." But the emphasis was on all kinds: the many-armed Shiva, a corpulent meditating Buddha, an Iroquois mask.

Theron felt like he was in a museum, not a home. He'd never encountered such pluralism before. He asked Roger what he believed in. He replied, "I don't know yet. We are Unitarians. My parents haven't forced any religion on me. When I reach my own conclusion, I will decide what is right for me." To Theron's assertion that Christianity is true, Roger simply replied, "It's true for you, but it might not be for me."

Roger's parents practiced a kind of democratic child rearing. They extended the "right to noninterference" to their child, creating a kind of separation of church and home. "We present the options and let the boy make up his own mind."

Roger's parents claimed a kind of neutrality toward religion. They claimed they were not imposing their values or preferences on their son. But weren't they? They taught their son that (1) he is the judge of what is true (not Jesus, the Bible, the church, or even his parents) and (2) that there really isn't any such thing as truth. Religion is about privately held values, preferences, and opinions. That is certainly a belief about God! Roger's parents feared the authority of Scripture, tradition, and even reason. In classic Emersonian fashion, they wanted him to learn to trust his intuitions and perspectives.

This view of authority represents a tradition of its own, one that will most likely make Roger one more "unencumbered self." It is also diametrically opposed to Christianity. In Ephesians 6, St. Paul writes, "Children, obey your parents in the Lord, for this is right. 'Honor your father and mother' (this is the first commandment with a promise), 'that it may be well with you and that you may live long on the earth.'"

If we are not taught how to honor these first and most important people in our lives, how and when will we ever learn to honor anyone, or how will we ourselves become honorable? Honor is one of the ingredients of love. Honor is a quality of character necessary for joyous, fulfilling, nurturing, productive relationships, both with God and our neighbors. If we think of heaven as a community of love, one of the virtues the Spirit of God will be developing in us so we can be part of that communion is honor.

In the *Book of Common Prayer*'s marriage rite, as a couple exchanges rings they say to one another, "With all that I am, and all that I have, I honor you." To honor someone else is a form of worship. It is to give of one's very best to the other. It is to care for the other in such a way that one always wants the very best for the other. To honor someone is a form of obedience: to listen to them fully, to trust their experience and expertise, to give them their due.

A child's first neighbor is his or her parents. In the last fifty to seventy-five years, the family has undergone a major transformation on many levels. Parents have gotten the idea that they exist for their children and that they shouldn't expect much of anything from them. John Rosemond, a syndicated columnist on child rearing writes:

Within the child-centered family, the implicit understanding is that the children are the most important people in the family, and the parent-child relationship is the most important relationship. And the more child-centered the American family has become, the more demandingly self-centered American children have become. And the more demanding children have become, the more demanding the task of raising them has become.[30]

Rosemond is not recommending a "Mommie Dearest" scenario. He is not saying child labor in the mines and sweatshops was a good thing. He is not in favor of "Dad is the king, and the whole family exists to please the king." St. Paul wrote, after commanding children to obey and honor their parents, "Fathers, do not provoke your children to anger, but bring them up in the discipline and instruction of the Lord" (Eph. 6:4 NASB). Another translation (NIV) says, "do not exasperate your children." In other words, parents are called to honor their children even as they train them to honor.

An Authority Problem: Reprise

The "family" is a crucial test case for our proposal.[31] Throughout the Bible the family certainly plays a central role. Sexual difference, marriage, childbearing—all are things God called good. A strong and intact family, nuclear or extended, is in many ways the basis for a just and peaceful society.[32] Yet, the family does not have inherent dignity, any more than does the individual. Starting with Cain and Abel the trouble begins, and it grows up to become the "city of man" and the "whore of Babylon."

The biblical tradition always put limits on the extent of familial loyalty and on obedience. The nations of the world will be blessed through Abram and Sarai, sojourners, and their joke of an heir (Isaac means laughter). This blessing begins with God's election of Israel. Israel should not take its election as a right, but as a gift. Israel is to be a witness and a blessing to the nations. The family also always was under Torah, the instruction for life in the covenant. To be a "child of God" always entailed obedience.[33]

The book of 1 Samuel, for instance, opens with dynasty trouble. Eli's sons are venal and corrupt. So God cuts them off and chooses a boy born of a barren woman to be a prophet. If Israel can have this problem with the children of priests, just imagine kings. Later, even as God promises to build David a house forever, that promise comes with a warning: He will punish his sons for their sins (see 2 Sam. ch. 7). So to this day, Judaism's adult passage rite is called a bar/bat mitzvah (son/daughter of the commandments). To be a full member of the family/community is to take personal, adult responsibility for keeping Torah.[34]

Jesus raises the stakes with his famous "He who loves father or mother more than me is not worthy of me; and he who loves son or daughter more than me is not worthy of me" (Matt. 10:37). Then of course is Jesus' reply to the message that his mother and brothers have come to collect him (because he must be crazy), "Who are my mother and my brothers? . . . Whoever does the will of God is my brother, and sister, and mother"(Mark 3:31–35). So one of the Ten Commandments (repeated and expanded by Paul) is to honor our parents; and at the same time, the kingdom, personified in Jesus, trumps family and parents. In short, the family is relativized vis-à-vis the kingdom.[35]

So what would legitimate authority look like? The only Christian rationality for authority is that it conform to the image of Christ Jesus, "who, though he was in the form of God, did not count equality with God a thing to be grasped, but emptied himself, taking the form of a servant" (Phil. 2:6–7). There must always be a sense that bearing authority is a gift and a responsibility, never a private possession or a right. Augustine spends some time on 1 Timothy 3:1, "He that desireth the episcopate desireth a good work." "He [Paul] wished to show that the episcopate is the title of a work, not of an honour. . . . So that he who loves to govern rather than to do good is no bishop."[36] Our lion is a lamb who was slain (Rev. 5:5–6).

Authority must always live within a whole host of limits. Authority is something one bears in one's person for the sake of the community. While honoring communities, families, institutions, and traditions, those who bear authority must always keep in mind that they are sojourners and those under them are sojourners. Nothing in the earthly city is a final destination. With that in mind, we can look at a few specifics.

Authorities are entrusted with the task of passing on the tradition. They make sure the gatherings happen in the right way, that all are present, and that the key stories get told. They watch the boundaries too, protecting the stories and incorporating new ones, approving marriages, giving moral guidance and correction to the young, and so on. Traditions are not acquired on the Internet or in an academic environment. They are handed over by one person to be received by another. Reception is a matter not simply of taking in knowledge, but of communion. As James McClendon said, "I want my students to grow up to become just like me . . . each in his or her own way."[37]

Authorities also are supposed to be living examples, individual embodiments of the soul of the community. Rabbi Judah Loew of Prague said, "For the scholar is like the Torah itself . . . and in its image. . . . And as the Holy One, may he be blessed, decreed and gave the Torah to all of Israel, so he gave us the sages, and they are also the essence of Torah."[38] Jesus says something quite similar when he says, "I am the way, and the truth, and the life. No one comes to the Father, but by me" (John 14:6).

The emotional leader is essential to any community. Families can disintegrate when a patriarch or matriarch dies. Unless the emotional center, the soul-bearing person, blesses their children, passing on that animus, the tradition will soon fade away. So the blessing always comes with a task, a vocation. The disciples of Jesus are mysteriously elected (no social contract among the Twelve) and are charged with making disciples, baptizing them in the name of the Triune God. Jesus sends, but he also creates a community. His Spirit draws the best out of each individual, that each one might become a person in community. To bear authority is to look out for the common good.

Existing for the common good is fraught with suffering. Danny Saunders's father was in many ways an autocrat. However, his Hasidic community trusted him deeply, and rightfully so, because he belonged to them all. He knew that the person bearing the most authority, paradoxically, had the least power. One of the ironies in the life of Oral Roberts is that his authority as a faith-healer is grounded in his own healing from tuberculosis, and even carried through to great pain in his shoulders because they were worn out from laying hands on people. Jesus is abundantly clear that his authority is a gift from his Father, and as we know so well, his lordship is demonstrated in his suffering for the life of the world.

In traditional iconography, the disciples are shown gathered around Jesus as a eucharistic community, and as apostles sent out two by two. Jesus gives the gospel, which must be handed over and received, person by person. Jesus also gathers a community, which embodies all that the gospel is. Baptism and Eucharist are holy moments when, in the Spirit, the church acts like what it is supposed to be, a communion of love.[39]

Epilogue

Diasporas and St. Augustine vs. The Architects of Babel

The United States, it goes almost without saying, is a nation of diasporas. All of us, except the remnant Native American population, descended from some migration; and even the Native American, who has experienced such dislocation and conquest, can speak of a "diasporic" past. Of all these groups, one still enjoys what we could call "hegemonic" status: the group made up of those of Western European descent. A mark of its historic privileged status is that it has not regarded itself as an ethnic group. The term *ethnic* has been reserved for all other diasporas (African, Asian, Latin American) and even for those who trace their roots back to the non-Western-European nations (the Italians, the Poles, etc.).

But no one, in fact, can lack tradition or ethnicity; people's roots may be shallow, diffuse, and unarticulated, but they can never be altogether absent. The question is not *whether* to be ethnic and traditional, but *how* one is to be these things. We have envisioned, in response, a place in which all cultures (including that of the church as an ecclesial culture-of-many-cultures) acknowledge their status as cultural minorities and their proper location as borderlands residents. In a real sense, we are all minorities now. And this is not a bad thing.

To argue that the church should embrace its borderlands location—and that no group should inhabit the "center"—is to speak in the Augustinian tradition. It is to argue for the limits of power, which is at the same time legitimate, God-given, *and* prone to abuse in human hands. It is to argue for a nation in which no one group (ethnic, religious, corporate, or bureaucratic) monopolizes power.

Our human quest to monopolize power (what Augustine called the *libido dominandi*) shows up in both Constantinianism and in modern liberalism. It is our Tower of Babel instinct. It is the instinct to build the earthly city as if it were the heavenly one. God's judgment on that hubris is the confusion of language—language being the instrument we use to shape and map our lives.

The dangerous assumption that we make is that if we just do it the right way, we can somehow get around the curse of confusion. We assume that Pentecost means God's judgment on the Tower of Babel is no longer in effect. The Constantinian mindset that persists within the church looks for a deep unity between earthly and heavenly cities—an application of Christian principles that will bring a definitive end to the strife and confusion between the nations. Christendom, no less than classical liberalism, sought to bypass God's judgment on Babel.

But pluralistic strife remains a persistent fact of life.

To embrace the empirical fact of pluralism is not to bless it or to sink into a quagmire of relativism. We simply acknowledge that we are under God's judgment. We are not saying truth is plural. We are not recommending the old proverb of the blind man describing an elephant. We simply acknowledge that utopia is—short of the *eschaton*—literally *nowhere*, and that anyone who claims they can build it is one of Babel's engineers.

The self-imposed ghetto is Babel-writ-small. As it rejects "the world," it invariably claims a totality for itself—even in its most

benign and nonviolent forms. It forgets the tares in the midst
of its own wheat, and the "throwbacks" among the "keepers"
in its fishing net. The Tower of Babel can look like a cathedral
or a meetinghouse in the round.

McWorld denies it is a Tower project. But the global village
we are supposed to be so happy about is about as Babelesque
as it gets. No, it does not look like the ancient ziggurat. But
the monopolistic power of golden arches, mouse ears, and super-
centers is the earthly city's hubris at its most bland and banal.

For what do McWorld and the modern ghetto have in common
if not the monopolistic concentration of power (in corporate hands
in the first case, with local autocrats in the second)? The space
that steers a clear course between McWorld and the ghetto—so
difficult to navigate in our individualistic culture—is the space
where power is held accountable and in check. It is a place where
traditions and communal authorities help us navigate between the
twin siren songs that call us to build a Tower of Babel. It is a place
that sustains festivals, pilgrimages, and transnational bridges. It
is a place that values and sustains the memories and hopes of all
its diasporas, not just those of its "self-made" individuals. Such
a land would be more hospitable to the life of the church, whose
well-being is part and parcel of everything that is particular.

And it might even be a place with more freedom, more peace,
and more justice—a place worth envisioning. The creation is,
after all, God's good creation. The result of God's judgment
on Babel was not utter chaos. Common cause can be found,
bridges for peace can be built—always in an ad hoc, negotiated
fashion.

As for the church itself, the difference between it and all other
cultures is that its members know themselves to be sojourners in
this earthly city, with hearts "restless till they rest in God."[1] And
St. Paul reminds us that Christians are spiritual descendants of
Abraham. We would do well to reclaim an ancient prayer, offered
by Israelites as they gave their tithe: "'A wandering Aramean was
my father: and he went down to Egypt and sojourned there'"

(Deut. 26:5). St. Paul brings this pilgrim sensibility to the church when he calls us, not just to tithe, but to present our bodies "as a living sacrifice, holy and acceptable to God, which is [our] spiritual worship," and to be "not . . . conformed to this world" (Rom. 12:1–2). To be a people of faith is to become strangers and aliens, to remember we work here under permit, under the proverbial Green Card.

And the church is called not just to be a resident alien group, but a place of welcome and care for the dispossessed: "'You shall not wrong a stranger or oppress him, for you were strangers in the land of Egypt'" (Exod. 22:21); "Do not neglect to show hospitality to strangers, for thereby some have entertained angels unawares" (Heb. 13:2). By claiming its pilgrim heritage, and by practicing that most pilgrim of virtues (hospitality), the church will be neither a ghetto (a walled enclave) nor a domesticated resort (sentimental but devoid of life) but an *inn* for weary travelers of the borderlands/frontiers, and an *outpost of hope* for exiles bound for the city of God.

Notes

Introduction

1. Benjamin Barber, *Jihad vs. McWorld: How Globalism and Tribalism Are Reshaping the World* (New York: Ballantine, 1995), p. 4.

2. The term *melting pot* did not originate with, but credit for its widespread popularity can be attributed to, Israel Zangwill's 1908 play, *The Melting Pot*. Interestingly, this term was used by Jews to speak to the very specific issue of Jewish immigration. Moreover, Jews, perhaps more than any other group, were capable of being both "white" and "different" (as opposed to the native populations, blacks, and Chinese). See David Biale, "The Melting Pot and Beyond: Jews and the Politics of American Identity," in *Insider/Outsider: American Jews and Multiculturalism,* ed. D. Biale, Galchinsky, and Heschel (Berkeley and Los Angeles: University of California Press, 1998), pp. 18–19.

3. A poignant example of the non-neutrality of the melting pot is Zangwill's play. "The most basic tension in *The Melting Pot* lies in the contrast between the play's assimilationist message and its specifically Jewish content. . . . As is often the case, Zangwill's cosmopolitanism turned out to be something like a form of Jewish particularism. . . . the end product is turn all true Americans into Jews" (ibid., pp. 19, 21).

4. This definition is taken from *The American Heritage Dictionary* (Boston: Houghton Mifflin, 1980).

5. J. Hector St. John de Crèvecoeur, *Letters from an American Farmer,* Letter 3: "What Is an American?" in *The Norton Anthology of American Literature,* 6th ed., ed. Nina Baym et al. (New York: Norton, 2002), p. 265.

6. Ibid.

7. Ibid., p. 269.

8. This textbook definition of the term *liberalism* is not the one that prevails in popular usage, but it is the one assumed by "communitarian" philosophers

like Michael Sandel and Alasdair MacIntyre—as well as in most other parts of the world.

9. We are not suggesting relativism here, but rather the conviction that truth is accessed "through a glass darkly" and that there is no neutral or bias-free vantage point from which a human being can speak.

10. See Kenneth Craycraft, *The American Myth of Religious Freedom* (Dallas: Spence, 1999), pp. 146–64.

11. See Biale, Galchinsky, and Heschel, *Insider/Outsider,* p. 1.

12. Ibid.

13. Soto is featured in the video titled *Hispanics in the U.S.* (part of the Films for the Humanities series *The Americas,* narrated by Raul Julia, 1992).

14. See Cornel West, *Race Matters* (New York: Vintage, 1994), p. 20. West argues for the urgent task of "speaking to the profound sense of psychological depression, personal worthlessness and social despair" present in these neighborhoods.

15. This is the main thrust of Linda Chavez's *Out of the Barrio: Toward a New Politics of Hispanic Assimilation* (New York: Basic Books, 1991).

16. Barber, *Jihad vs. McWorld,* p. 9.

17. Ibid., p. 4.

18. Ibid., p. 11.

19. This same form of fast-track liberalism is also advocated by some Kennedy-era left-liberals such as Arthur Schlesinger.

20. Biale, Galchinsky, and Heschel, in *Insider/Outsider,* champions an individually chosen identity built on multiculturalist ideals (pp. 29–32).

21. See Rodney Clapp, *A Peculiar People: The Church as Culture in a Post-Christian Society* (Downers Grove, Ill.: InterVarsity Press, 1996), pp. 16–21.

22. See Jeffrey Stout, *Ethics after Babel: The Languages of Morals and Their Discontents* (Boston: Beacon, 1988), pp. 1–2.

23. Ibid., p. 189.

24. See Walter Breuggemann, *Genesis in Interpretation: A Bible Commentary for Teaching and Preaching,* ed. James L. Mays (Atlanta: John Knox, 1982), pp. 97–104.

25. Frank R. VanDevelder, *The Biblical Journey of Faith: The Road of the Sojourner* (Philadelphia: Fortress, 1988), p. 23.

26. Augustine, *The City of God,* trans. and ed. Marcus Dods (New York: Random House, 1993), book 11, chapter 1.

27. "The Epistle to Diognetus," in *The Apostolic Fathers,* ed. J. B. Lightfoot and J. R. Harmer (Grand Rapids: Baker, 1984; reprt. from 1891 ed., London: Macmillan), paragraph 5, pp. 505–6. According to Lightfoot, the likely date for the letter is around A.D. 150; its author is unknown.

28. See Mitchell Cohen, "In Defense of Shaatnez: A Politics for Jews in a Multicultural America," in *Insider/Outsider: American Jews and Multiculturalism,* ed. D. Biale, Galchinsky, and Heschel (Los Angeles: University of California Press, 1998), pp. 34–54.

29. See Frederick W. Weidmann, "To Sojourn" or "To Dwell," in *Reading in Christian Communities: Essays on Interpretation in the Early Church,* ed. Charles Bobertz and David Brakke (Notre Dame, Ind.: University of Notre Dame Press, 2002), pp. 29–40. "In his study of 1st Peter, John Elliott reminds the modern reader that, 'Politically and legally, persons did not become *paroikoi* because of their conversion to Christianity but as a result of a change in their geographical and legal status.' Given the imperial bureaucratic structure of the day, that is most certainly true. Elliott concludes that Christian use of 'sojourn' may 'have both literal and metaphorical connotations. In any case, it 'draws its rhetorical power from the actuality of lived experience.' Specifically, 'from the perspective of 1st Peter the basic point is that conversion involved no alleviation of the predicament of social alienation but rather its intensification'; further, 'this situation of social and cultural alienation' is 'similar to that experienced by ancient Israel'" (p. 30, referring to John Elliott, *A Home for the Homeless: A Social-Scientific Criticism of 1st Peter, Its Situation and Strategy* [Minneapolis: Fortress, 1990], pp. xxix–xxx).

30. In Lightfoot and Harmer, *Apostolic Fathers,* p. 203.

31. Jews have been and continue to be the ultimate insider/outsiders in America. They have benefited from and advocated the melting pot more than any other group; at the same time they have resisted assimilation more than any other immigrant group. "Identification and integration with the majority stands at odds with the Jews' equal desire to preserve their identity as a minority. Never before have Jews confronted so powerfully the tension between maintaining continuity with tradition and reinventing Jewish life so that it fully meets women's needs for justice and equity" (Biale, Galchinsky, and Heschel, *Insider/Outsider,* p. 5).

Chapter 1

1. The article titled, "Retribution Sank Nomination, Chavez Says," was posted on the Web at cnn.com on January 9, 2001.

2. Chavez's recently published memoir, *An Unlikely Conservative: The Transformation of an Ex-Liberal* (New York: Basic Books, 2002), opens with a more detailed description of the nomination process and the events that led up to it. Her account is aimed more at presenting herself as the victim of a political double standard than at reflecting on some of the cultural issues raised by the situation.

3. Rodriguez has exchanged his public role on the *MacNeil/Lehrer NewsHour* for an editorial one at the *New York Times.*

4. Richard Rodriguez, *Hunger of Memory* (New York: Bantam, 1983), pp. 19–20.

5. Ibid., p. 12.

6. Ibid., pp. 35–36.

7. Ibid., p. 30.

8. See Roger Lundin, *The Culture of Interpretation: Christian Faith and the Postmodern World* (Grand Rapids: Eerdmans, 1993). Lundin argues throughout the book that Emerson's contempt for tradition has dominated much of American thought, from his time up through postmodern deconstructionism.

9. Rodriguez, *Hunger of Memory,* p. 107.

10. In *A Peculiar People: The Church as Culture in a Post-Christian Society* (Downers Grove, Ill.: InterVarsity Press, 1996), pp. 58–65, Rodney Clapp argues that as far back as the nineteenth century, the church followed some of the era's leading intellectuals (such as Matthew Arnold) in a motion of cultural retreat into a hallowed-but-marginal domestic space. This domesticating process is most evident here in Rodriguez.

11. Rodriguez, *Hunger of Memory,* p. 107.

12. Ibid., p. 110.

13. Kenneth Craycraft devotes the third chapter of *The American Myth of Religious Freedom* (Dallas: Spence, 1999), to developing this idea of freedom as a relative concept.

14. Richard Rodriguez, *Days of Obligation: An Argument with My Mexican Father* (New York: Penguin, 1993), p. 197.

15. Ibid., p. xvi.

16. See Ilan Stavans, *The Hispanic Condition* (New York: Harper Collins, 1995), pp. 61–91.

17. Ibid., p. 61

18. Ibid., p. 57.

19. Ibid., pp. 1–25.

20. Richard Rodriguez, *Brown: The Last Discovery of America* (New York: Viking, 2002), p. xi.

21. Ibid., p. 52.

22. Rodriguez, *Days of Obligation*, pp. xvi–xvii.

23. See Octavio Paz, *The Labyrinth of Solitude* (New York: Ballantine, 1960), p. 12, where he states, "I should confess that many of the reflections in this essay occurred to me outside of Mexico. During a two-year stay in the United States."

24. Ibid., p. 339. Paz states that in colonial Mexico the *ejido* (communal peasant landholding) "coexisted with the large colonial estate and the Church's enormous landholdings."

25. Ibid., p. 341.

26. Ibid., p. 361.

27. Ibid., p. 47.

28. Ibid., p. 21.

29. Rodriguez, *Brown,* p. xi.

30. Ibid., p. 224.

31. This is the endorsement on the back cover of our edition of *Days of Obligation,* written by Enrique Fernandez of the *Village Voice.*

32. H. Richard Niebuhr, *Christ and Culture* (New York: Harper and Row, 1951), pp. 83–84.

33. Timothy Phillips and Dennis Okholm, *Welcome to the Family: An Introduction to Evangelical Christianity* (Grand Rapids: Baker, 1996), p. 204.

Chapter 2

1. This question is an adaptation of Alasdair MacIntyre's famous question and book title, *Whose Justice? Which Rationality?* (Notre Dame, Ind.: University of Notre Dame Press, 1988).

2. Nia Vardalos, *My Big Fat Greek Wedding* (Home Box Office, 2002).

3. *Fiddler on the Roof*, dir. Norman Jewison (MGM, 1971).

4. J. Hector St. John de Crèvecoeur, *Letters from an American Farmer*, Letter #3: "What Is an American?" in *The Norton Anthology of American Literature*, 6th ed., ed. Nina Baym et. al. (New York: Norton, 2002), p. 265.

5. See Sholom Aleichem, *Tevya and His Daughters; A Play in Two Acts*, trans. Arnold Perl (Dramatists Play Service, 1998).

6. Jaroslav Pelikan related this statement of Altman's to begin his Jefferson Lecture entitled *The Vindication of Tradition* (New Haven: Yale University Press, 1984), p. 3.

7. Stephen Toulmin, *Cosmopolis: The Hidden Agenda of Modernity* (Chicago: University of Chicago Press, 1990), p. 75.

8. John Locke, *A Letter concerning Toleration*, ed. James H. Tully (Indianapolis: Hackett, 1983), 23, in Kenneth Craycraft, *The American Myth of Religious Freedom* (Dallas: Spence, 1999), p. 44.

9. Stanley Fish (*The Trouble with Principle* [Cambridge: Harvard University Press, 1999], pp. 165–66) summarizes Locke's thought, and comments on liberalism:

[According to Locke,] "Citizens, in short, are to be treated equally no matter what opinions they believe and profess, and they should neither be deprived of worldly advantage nor given a greater share of it because they hold those opinions rather than others. If this sounds familiar, it is because what we have here, already fully articulated in 1689, is the basic structure of liberal political theory: a firm distinction between the public and the private realms (underwritten by a distinction between body and soul/mind and a determination to patrol the boundaries between them so that secular authorities will not penalize citizens for the thoughts they have [no thought control] or the opinions they express [no censorship], and religious authorities will not meddle in the worldly affairs of their parishioners [no theocracy])."

10. Pelikan, *Vindication of Tradition*, p. 43.

11. Stanley Hauerwas (from Cornel West from Sydney Ahlstrom), *With the Grain of the Universe: The Church's Witness and Natural Theology* (Grand Rapids: Brazos, 2001), p. 81.

12. *The Reader's Companion to World Literature,* 2d ed., rev. and updated, ed. Lillian Hornstein, Leon Edel, and Horst Frenz; Calvin Brown, gen. ed. (New York: New American Library, 1973), p. 173.

13. Pelikan, *Vindication of Tradition,* p. 66.

14. Ralph Waldo Emerson, in *The Best of Ralph Waldo Emerson: Essays, Poems, Addresses* (Roslyn, N.Y.: W. J. Black, 1941), p. 22.

15. Ibid., p. 42.

16. This section on William James is based on the work of Stanley Hauerwas in *With the Grain of the Universe,* pp. 43–86.

17. Hauerwas writes in *With the Grain of the Universe,* James thought that after Darwin it was impossible to think that the world represented an orderly order. That we exist is an accident, and our ending will be equally accidental. Chance, not purpose, rules. Accordingly, science itself can no longer offer certainty and/or proof but only probable and persuasive explanations" (p. 49). Given the randomness of existence, "A man's religious faith is essentially his faith in the existence of an unseen order of some kind in which the riddles of the natural order may be found and explained. . . . 'Religion' is simply James's way of naming the fact that our minds are teleological mechanisms that constitute our difference from brutes" (Cornel West, *The American Evasion of Philosophy: A Geneology of Pragmatism* (Madison: University of Wisconsin Press, 1989], pp. 59–60). What James did in *The Varieties of Religious Experience* was "the piling up of religious narratives . . . to show that religion is but another name for the hope necessary to sustain a modest humanism" (p. 63).

18. Ibid., pp. 82–83.

19. George A. Lindbeck, *The Nature of Doctrine: Religion and Theology in a Postliberal Age* (Philadelphia: Westminster, 1984). Lindbeck takes up the discussion at the turn of the nineteenth century with Kant, and especially with Schleiermacher. "In Schleiermacher's case, it will be recalled, the source of all religion is in the 'feeling of absolute dependence,' but there are many and significantly different ways of describing the basic religious experience, as is illustrated by a succession of influential theories of religion stretching from Schleiermacher through Rudolf Otto to Mircea Eliade and beyond. Nevertheless, whatever the variations, thinkers of this tradition all locate ultimately significant contact with whatever is finally important to religion in the prereflective experiential depths of the self and regard the public or outer features of religion as expressive and evocative objectifications (i.e., nondiscursive symbols) of internal experience. For nearly two hundred years this tradition has provided intellectually brilliant and empirically impressive accounts of the religious life that . . . have been at the heart of the romantic, idealistic, and phenomenological-existentialist streams of . . . Western culture. The habits of thought it has fostered are ingrained in the soul of the modern West, perhaps particularly in the souls of theologians" (p. 21).

20. The Reverend Matthew Gunter, private conversation.

21. Lindbeck, *Nature of Doctrine,* p. 22

22. Lindbeck wrote prior to September 11, 2001: "Many argue that given the evolutionary forces of change, the centripetal forces of individualism, and religious pluralism, we have no choice but 'experiential-expressivism'" (ibid., p. 21).

23. Pelikan, *Vindication of Tradition*, p. 5.

24. Ibid., p. 18.

25. Ibid., p. 65.

26. Ibid., pp. 65–66.

27. Pelikan writes, "For the dichotomy between tradition and insight breaks down under the weight of history itself. A 'leap of progress' is not a standing broad jump, which begins at the line of where we are now; it is a running broad jump through where we have been to where we go next. The growth of insight—in science, in the arts, in philosophy and theology—has not come through progressively sloughing off more and more of tradition, as though insight would be purest and deepest when it has finally freed itself of the dead past. It simply has not worked that way in the history of the tradition, and it does not work that way now. By including the dead in the circle of discourse, we enrich the quality of the conversation" (ibid., p. 81).

28. Pelikan's claim that advances in science are also part of the tradition process is not made in a vacuum. Thomas Kuhn's *The Structure of Scientific Revolutions* (1962) broke Descartes's lock on science. Stephen Toulmin also worked on this subject, and even before Kuhn, so we turn to him for insight on how science realized it is a kind of tradition too.

29. Toulmin, *Cosmopolis*, p. 84.

30. Alasdair MacIntyre, *After Virtue: A Study in Moral Theory*, 2d ed. (Notre Dame, Ind.: University of Notre Dame Press, 1984), p. 22.

31. The very way Lindbeck talks about Enlightenment rationalism belies this massive shift in thought. "Whatever the variations, thinkers of this *tradition* all locate ultimately significant contact with whatever is finally important to religion, in the prereflective experiential depths of the self, and regard the public or outer features of religion as expressive and evocative objectifications (i.e., nondiscursive symbols) of internal experience" (*The Nature of Doctrine*, p. 21, emphasis added). Experiential expressivism is not self-relevant truth, but a tradition or method.

32. Fish incisively says, "If the difference is fundamental—that is, touches basic beliefs and commitments—how can you respect it without disrespecting your own beliefs and commitments? And on the other side, do you really show respect for a view by tolerating it, as you might tolerate the buzzing of a fly? Or do you show respect when you take it seriously enough to oppose it? . . . In an intellectual disagreement the parties can talk to one another because they share a set of basic assumptions; but in a fundamental disagreement, basic assumptions are precisely what is in dispute" (*Trouble with Principle*, pp. 66–67).

33. Stated by Bruce S. Thornton in an interview with Ken Myers, Mars Hill Audio (Charlottesville, Va.), vol. 50, May/June 2001.

34. What we are left with, then, is Nietzsche of whom MacIntyre writes, "If there is nothing to morality but expressions of will, my morality can only be what my will creates. There can be no place for such fictions as natural rights, utility, the greatest happiness of the greatest number. I myself must now bring into existence 'new tables of what is good'. [Nietzsche, in *The Gay Science* (section 335), writes:] 'We, however, *want to become those we are*—human beings who are new, unique, incomparable, who give themselves laws, who create themselves.' [This is what Emerson would sound like if he were as crazy as Nietzsche.] The rational and rationality justifies autonomous moral subject of the eighteenth century is a fiction, an illusion; so, Nietzsche resolves, let will replace reason and let us make ourselves into autonomous moral subjects by some gigantic and heroic act of the will. . . . For it is in his relentlessly serious pursuit of the problem, not in his frivolous solutions that Nietzsche's greatness lies, the greatness that makes him *the* moral philosopher *if* the only alternatives to Nietzsche's moral philosophy turn out to be those formulated by the philosophers of the Enlightenment and their successors" (*After Virtue*, pp. 113–14). A few pages later MacIntyre challenges the accepted "truth" of the Enlightenment project. "What then the conjunction of philosophical and historical argument reveals is that *either* one must follow through the aspirations and the collapse of the different versions of the Enlightenment project until there remains only the Nietzschean diagnosis and the Nietzschean problematic or one must hold that the Enlightenment project was not only mistaken, but should never have been commenced in the first place. There is no third alternative and more particularly there is no alternative provided by those thinkers at the heart of the contemporary conventional curriculum in moral philosophy" (p. 118).

35. MacIntyre, *After Virtue*, p. 222.

36. N. T. Wright "Jesus and the Quest," in *The Truth about Jesus,* ed. Donald Armstrong (Grand Rapids: Eerdmans, 1998), pp. 8–9.

37. N. T. Wright, *What St. Paul Really Said: Was Paul of Tarsus the Real Founder of Christianity?* (Grand Rapids: Eerdmans, 1997), p. 45.

38. Lesslie Newbigin, *Foolishness to the Greeks: The Gospel and Western Culture* (Grand Rapids: Eerdmans, 1986), p. 124.

39. Miroslav Volf ("Theology for a Way of Life," in *Practicing Theology: Beliefs and Practices in Christian Life,* ed. Miroslav Volf and Dorothy Bass [Grand Rapids: Eerdmans, 2002], pp. 245–63) writes, "Core Christian beliefs are by definition normatively inscribed in sacraments but not in 'practices.' Hence sacraments ritually enact normative patterns for practices"(p. 248).

40. Volf writes, "The sacrament of the Lord's Supper itself is very much a summary of the whole of Christian life, at whose heart lies the self-giving of God for sinful humanity, and the eschatological Feast is the sum of Christian hopes for communion between the Triune God and God's glorified people" (ibid., p. 249).

41. Volf speaks of an *"as-so"* structure to Christian practices. *"As* God has received us in Christ, *so* we too are to receive our fellow human beings" (ibid., p. 250). "Basic Christian beliefs *as beliefs* entail practical commitments. These commitments may need to be explicated so as to become clear, or they may need to be connected to specific issues in concrete situations, but they don't need to be *added* to the beliefs; they inhere in the beliefs. Christian beliefs are not simply statements about what was, is, and will be the case; they are statements about what *should* be the case and what human beings should do about that" (ibid., pp. 253–54).

42. Ephraim Radner ("Doctrine, Destiny, and the Figure of History," in *Reclaiming Faith: Essays on Orthodoxy in the Episcopal Church and the Baltimore Declaration*, ed. Ephraim Radner and George Sumner [Grand Rapids: Eerdmans, 1993], pp. 66–71) speaks of a basic New Testament ethic in which Christians and the church are to *conform* to the *figure* of Jesus Christ.

43. Volf, "Theology for a Way of Life," p. 255.

44. Pelikan, *Vindication of Tradition,* p. 41.

45. See John Howard Yoder, "The Authority of Tradition," in *The Priestly Kingdom: Social Ethics as Gospel* (Notre Dame, Ind.: University of Notre Dame Press, 1984).

46. Robert Wilken, *The Christians as the Romans Saw Them* (New Haven: Yale University Press, 1984); see especially chapter 3, "The Piety of the Persecutors."

47. Ralph Waldo Emerson, "Self-Reliance," in *Emerson's Essays,* Everyman's Library, vol. 12, ed. Ernest Rhys (London: J. M. Dent; New York: E. P. Dutton, 1906), p. 31.

48. Ralph Waldo Emerson, "Divinity School Address," in Emerson, *Best of*, p. 42.

49. Rowan Greer, *Broken Lights and Mended Lives: Theology and Common Life in the Early Church* (University Park: Pennsylvania State University Press, 1986), p. 26.

50. This section on Irenaeus is based on ibid., pp. 24–43.

51. Justo González: *The Story of Christianity,* vol. 1 (San Francisco: Harper and Row, 1984), pp. 62–66. Jaroslav Pelikan, in *The Vindication of Tradition,* talks about the place of tradition in the life of the church in the patristic period. He captures the sense that tradition is a sort of living organism. "From the Church Fathers of the 4th century, John Henry Newman knew that the public doxology . . . was practically a test of faith. . . . The authentic tradition of orthodoxy was not a matter to be decided by an intellectually formulated 'rule of faith' set forth by scholars and theologians, but by the 'rule of prayer' of the thousands of silent believers, who worshipped in spirit and in truth" (p. 30).

52. Greer, p. 4.

53. See Greer, pp. 4–5.

54. See Richard B. Hays, *The Moral Vision of the New Testament: Community, Cross, New Creation: A Contemporary Introduction to New Testament Ethics* (New York: HarperCollins, 1996), pp. 304–306.

55. Fish, *Trouble with Principle*, pp. 93–114.

56. In Roger Lundin, *Culture of Interpretation: Christian Faith and the Postmodern World* (Grand Rapids: Eerdmans, 1993), p. 219.

57. This definition of the ideal American was taken from R. W. B. Lewis, *The American Adam: Innocence, Tragedy, and Tradition in the Nineteenth Century*, cited in ibid., p. 228.

58. See Yoder, *Priestly Kingdom*, pp. 69, 76.

59. In Pelikan, *Vindication of Tradition*, p. 82.

60. Irenaeus, "Against Heresies," 3. 24, in *Early Biblical Interpretation*, James L. Kugel and Rowan A. Greer (Philadelphia: Westminster, 1986), p. 124.

61. Lesslie Newbigin, *The Gospel in a Pluralist Society* (Grand Rapids: Eerdmans, 1989), p. 50.

Chapter 3

1. See Paul Simon's song "The Coast," in *Rhythm of the Saints* (Warner Brothers, 1990).

2. Gustavo Pérez Firmat, *Life on the Hyphen: The Cuban-American Way* (Austin: University of Texas Press, 1994).

3. Oscar Hijuelos, *The Mambo Kings Play Songs of Love* (New York: Harper-Collins, 1989), pp. 406–407.

4. Pérez Firmat, *Life on the Hyphen*, p. 221.

5. Ibid., p. 5

6. See Mark Noll's *The Scandal of the Evangelical Mind* (Grand Rapids: Eerdmans, 1994). Chiding evangelicalism for being inhospitable to the life of the mind, Noll points out how fundamentalism both preserved evangelicalism against the corrosive forces of modernism and disfigured it in the process. This phenomenon is analogous to the exile mindset of the hard-line Cuban-American leadership, which has both preserved and disfigured the culture of the island.

7. Pérez Firmat, *Life on the Hyphen*, p. 5.

8. Ibid., pp. 126–30.

9. This article can be found online at pocho.com.

10. The term *McCondo,* coined by postmodern Chilean novelist Alberto Fuguet, is an irreverent hybrid of the terms *McWorld, condominium,* and *Macondo.* The latter is the archetypal Latin American town featured in Gabriel García Márquez's *One Hundred Years of Solitude.*

11. See the article "Gloria Estefan Speaks Her Mind" (1997, *Exito Online,* South Florida Interactive, Inc., and Sun-Sentinel Co.). A good portrait of how the exile leadership in Miami has created a violently McCarthyist political climate is given in Ann Louise Bardach's *Cuba Confidential: Love and Vengeance in Miami and Havana* (New York: Random House, 2002). The leadership's

hard-line stance, which was softening over the last decade, is bound to be revived by Castro's April 2003 crackdown on dissidents.

12. See "Gloria Estefan Speaks Her Mind."

13. For a good portrait of the Cuban musical tradition and its cultural significance, see Philip Sweeney's *The Rough Guide to Cuban Music* (London: Penguin, 2001).

14. See Andres Perez's online article "Gloria Estefan: Hija del Exilio—Daughter of the Exile" at http://www.fiu.edu/~fcf/yara/.

15. See the article "Cristina Garcia's *Dreaming in Cuban:* The Contested Domains of Politics, Family and History," in *U.S. Latino Literature: A Critical Guide,* ed. Harold Augenbraum and Margarite Fernández-Olmos (Westport, Conn.: Greenwood, 2000).

16. Cristina Garcia, *Dreaming in Cuban* (New York: Ballantine, 1992), p. 154.

17. Ibid., p. 235.

18. Mikhail Bakhtin, *The Dialogic Imagination* (Austin: University of Texas Press, 1981).

19. Ilan Stavans, "Sandra Cisneros: Form over Content," in *The Essential Ilan Stavans* (New York: Routledge, 2000), pp. 41–46. Assessing the general state of Latino literature in the United States, he asserts that "high-caliber figures like Oscar Hijuelos, Aristeo Brito and Cristina Garcia have already delivered commanding and mature novels, at once multifaceted and far-reaching, volumes that go beyond easy stereotypes."

20. Julia Alvarez, *How the Garcia Girls Lost Their Accents* (New York: Plume, 1992), p. 7.

21. Ibid., p. 22.

22. See Maxine Hong Kingston's *Woman Warrior: Memoirs of a Girlhood among Ghosts* (New York: Knopf, 1976).

23. H. Richard Niebuhr, *Christ and Culture* (New York: Harper and Row, 1951), pp. 149–89.

24. Timothy Phillips and Dennis Okholm, *Welcome to the Family: An Introduction to Evangelical Christianity* (Grand Rapids, Baker, 1996), p. 204.

Chapter 4

1. Robert Bellah, Richard Madsen, William Sullivan, Ann Swidler, and Steven Tipton, eds., *Habits of the Heart: Individualism and Commitment in American Life* (New York: Harper and Row, 1985), pp. 6, 23.

2. We are pointing out the way this un-tradition turns Alasdair MacIntyre's definition of tradition on its head. "A living tradition then is a historically extended, *socially embodied* argument and an argument precisely in part about the goods which constitute that tradition" (*After Virtue: A Study in Moral Theory,* 2d ed. (Notre Dame, Ind.: University of Notre Dame Press, 1984, p. 222, emphasis ours).

3. Jean-Jacques Rousseau, *The Social Contract,* in *Classics of Western Thought,* vol. 3, 3d ed., ed. Charles Hirschfield and Edgar Knobel (San Diego: Harcourt Brace Jovanovich, 1980), p. 190.

4. Rodriquez incarnates MacIntyre's idea on the relationship between tradition and community. MacIntyre writes on the way liberalism defines the human in opposition to tradition and community: "For liberal individualism a community is simply an arena in which individuals each pursue their own self-chosen conception of the good life, and political institutions exist to provide that degree of order which makes such self-determined activity possible" (*After Virtue,* p. 195). "From the standpoint of individualism I am what I myself choose to be" (p. 220).

5. Philip Rieff's work *The Triumph of the Therapeutic* (Chicago: Universtiy of Chicago Press, 1987): "The cultural revolution of therapy gives the unimpeded self 'a new way of using all commitments, which amounts to loyalty toward none'"(p. 200).

6. Bellah et al., *Habits of the Heart,* pp. 108–9.

7. We owe this insight to Diogenes Allen.

8. Bellah et al., *Habits of the Heart,* pp. 111–12.

9. Barbara Dafoe Whitehead, *The Divorce Culture: Rethinking Our Commitments to Marriage and Family* (New York: Vintage Books/Random House, 1996), p. 54.

10. Ibid., p. 67.

11. Ibid., pp. 13–18, 76–78.

12. See James Davison Hunter, *Culture Wars: The Struggle to Define America: Making Sense of the Battles over the Family, Art, Education, Law, and Politics* (New York: Basic Books, 1991), especially chapter 7.

13. Pipher writes, "Americans hold two parallel versions of the family—the idealized version and the dysfunctional version. The idealized version portrays families as wellsprings of love and happiness, loyal, wholesome and true. The dysfunctional version depicts families as disturbed and disturbing, and suggests that salvation lies in extricating oneself from all the ties that bind. . . . In the 1990s the dysfunctional version of family seems the most influential. This belief system goes along with the culture of narcissism, which sells people the idea that families get in the way of individual fulfillment. Currently, many Americans are deeply mistrustful of their own and other people's families. Pop psychology presents families as pathology-producing. Talk shows make families look like hotbeds of sin and sickness. Day after day people testify about the diverse forms of emotional abuse that they suffered in their families. Movies and television often portray families as useless impediments" (*The Shelter of Each Other: Rebuilding Our Families* [New York: Ballantine, 1996], p. 24).

14. Pipher writes, "In our culture, after a certain age, children no longer have permission to love their parents. We define adulthood as breaking away, disagreeing and making up new rules. Just when teenagers most need their parents, they are encouraged to distance from them. A friend told me of walk-

ing with her son in a shopping mall. They passed some of his friends and she noticed that suddenly he was ten feet behind, trying hard not to be seen with her. She said, 'I felt like I was drooling and wearing purple plaid polyester.' Later her son told her that he enjoyed being with her, but that his friends all hated their parents and he would be teased if anyone knew he loved her. He said, 'I'm confused about this. Am I supposed to hate you?'"(*Shelter*, pp. 24–25).

15. Pipher writes, "It's a common American belief that to be free of one's family is to be mentally healthy. Many tribes from all over the world believe that to be without family is to be without identity, to be dead. They are not far from wrong. An absolutely free self is an empty self. Families with all their inadequacies generally care for their members. In a communist country, without a family, a person has nothing between him/her and the state. In America, without a family, a person has nothing between him/her and the corporate consumer culture" (*Shelter*, p. 116).

16. Robert Frost, "The Death of the Hired Man," in *Robert Frost, Poetry and Prose*, ed. Edward Lathem and Lawrance Thompson (New York: Holt, Rinehart and Winston, 1972), p. 21.

17. Pipher writes, "For the first time in two thousand years of Western civilization, families live in houses without walls. That is, they live in a world in which walls offer no protection. Technology has brought the outside world into the living room. . . . The media forms our new community. The electronic village is our hometown. The old community of particular people in particular places and times who knew each other in a variety of ways over decades has been replaced. . . . Parents have no real community to back up the values that they try to teach their children. Family members may be in the same house, but they are no longer truly interacting. They may be in the same room, but instead of making their own story, they are watching another family's story unfold. Or even more likely, family members are separated, having private experiences with different electronic equipment" (pp. 12, 14).

18. Jean Bethke Elshtain, *Augustine and the Limits of Politics* (Notre Dame, Ind.: University of Notre Dame Press, 1995), p. 35.

19. Benjamin Barber, *Jihad vs. McWorld: How Globalism and Tribalism Are Reshaping the World* (New York: Ballantine, 1995), p. 223. (Barber attributes this insight to Alan Durnign without full citation.)

20. Barber writes, "If McWorld in its most elemental negative form is a kind of animal greed—one that is achieved by an aggressive and irresistible energy, Jihad in its most elemental negative form is a kind of animal fear propelled by anxiety in the face of uncertainty and relieved by self-sacrificing zealotry—an escape out of history.

Jihad tends the soul that McWorld abjures and strives for the moral well-being that McWorld, busy with the consumer choices it mistakes for freedom, disdains (*Jihad vs. McWorld*, p. 215).

21. Ibid., p. 24.

22. Barber writes, "Their [multinational corporations'] customers are not citizens of a particular nation or members of a parochial clan: they belong to the universal tribe of consumers defined by needs and wants that are ubiquitous, if not by nature, then by the cunning of advertising. A consumer is a consumer is a consumer" (ibid., p. 23).

23. Barber writes, "McWorld calls on us to see ourselves as private and solitary, interacting primarily via commercial transactions where 'me' displaces 'we'; and it permits private corporations whose only interest is their revenue stream to define by default the public goods of the individuals and communities they serve (ibid., p. 98).

24. See Robert P. Kraynak (*Christian Faith and Modern Democracy: God and Politics in the Fallen World* [Notre Dame, Ind.: University of Notre Dame Press, 2001]), who writes, "[His critique] is . . . a variation on the 'theory of mass society' that has been developed by the greatest social critics of the modern democratic age—who I would identify as Alexis de Tocqueville, Friedrich Nietzsche, and José Ortega y Gasset. In their analysis, the rise of modern democracy (along with modern science, industry, and technology) has unleashed the power and dynamism of the people while turning them into the anonymous 'masses'—an undifferentiated collection of rootless, traditionless, and isolated individuals, each claiming to be unique and special but in reality identical to each other in their mundane pursuits, seemingly free but in reality slavishly conformist and ripe for exploitation by new kinds of tyrants, both violent and banal. With the empowering of the masses comes the prospect of a new kind of democratic tyranny" (p. 29).

25. Barber writes, "Ironically, a world that is coming together pop culturally and commercially is a world whose discrete subnational ethnic and religious racial parts are also far more in evidence, in no small part as a reaction to McWorld" (*Jihad vs. McWorld,* p.11).

26. Ibid., p. 160.

27. Ibid., p. 216.

28. Chaim Potok, *The Chosen* (New York: Simon & Schuster, 1967).

29. Ibid., pp. 16–17.

30. Ibid., p. 26.

31. Ibid., p. 35.

32. Ibid., pp. 283–84.

33. Highlighting the liberal-myth side of Potok, Sheldon Grebstein comments on *The Chosen:* "Accordingly, the American cultural myth or fable at the heart of *The Chosen* is essentially that of both the Horatio Alger stories and *The Great Gatsby*—the dream of success. In this version the story is played out by an improbable but possible "only in America" cast of Hasidic and Orthodox Jews, who demonstrate that people can still make good through hard work, and that severe difficulties can be overcome by pluck, integrity, and dedication. At the story's end the novel's two young heroes are about to realize the reward they have earned: a limitless future. In sum, *The Chosen* can be interpreted

from this standpoint as an assertion of peculiarly American optimism and social idealism. Very simply, it says Yes" ("The Phenomenon of the Really Jewish Best Seller: Potok's *The Chosen*," in *Studies in American Jewish Literature* 1 [spring 1975]: 25).

34. "The Great American Novel" on *Only Visiting This Planet* (Verve, 1972).

35. Kallistos Ware, *The Orthodox Way*, rev. ed. (Crestwood, N.Y.: St. Vladimir's Seminary Press, 2001), p. 62.

36. John D. Zizioulas, *Being as Communion: Studies in Personhood and the Church* (Crestwood, N.Y.: St. Vladimir's Seminary Press, 1997), p. 18.

37. C. S. Lewis, *The Great Divorce* (New York: Macmillan, 1946).

38. Augustine, *City of God*, book 1, chapter 9.

39. Elshtain, *Augustine and the Limits of Politics*, p. 81.

40. William C. Placher, *Narratives of a Vulnerable God: Christ, Theology, and Scripture* (Louisville: Westminster/John Knox, 1994), p. 66.

41. Zizioulas, *Being as Communion*, p. 111.

42. Ibid., pp. 114–15.

43. William Willimon, *Worship as Pastoral Care* (Nashville: Abingdon, 1979), p. 171.

44. In ibid., p. 184.

45. In ibid.

46. Quoted in ibid., p. 186.

47. It's helpful to again consider Jaroslav Pelikan's comment: "From the Church Fathers of the 4th century, John Henry Newman knew that the public doxology . . . was practically a test of faith. . . . the authentic tradition of orthodoxy was not a matter to be decided by an intellectually formulated 'rule of faith' set forth by scholars and theologians, but by the 'rule of prayer' of the thousands of silent believers, who worshipped in spirit and in truth" (*The Vindication of Tradition*, [New Haven: Yale University Press, 1984], p. 30).

48. MacIntyre writes:

The story of my life is always embedded in the story of those communities from which I derive my identity. I am born with a past; and to try to cut myself off from that past, in the individualist mode, is to deform my present relationships. The possession of an historical identity and the possession of a social identity coincide. Notice that rebellion against my identity is always one possible mode of expressing it.

What I am, therefore, is in key part what I inherit, a specific past that is present to some degree in my present. I find myself part of a history and that is generally to say, whether I like it or not, whether I recognize it or not, one of the bearers of a tradition. (*After Virtue*, p. 221)

49. Chaim Potok, *The Book of Lights* (New York: Knopf, 1981).

50. Chaim Potok, *The Promise* (New York: Knopf, 1969).

51. Ibid., p. 266.

52. Ibid., p. 291.

53. Ibid., p. 331.

54. Kenneth Craycraft, *The American Myth of Religious Freedom* (Dallas: Spence, 1999), p. 65.

55. Fish writes, "'Laws are made for the government of actions, and while they may not interfere with mere religious belief and opinions, they may with practices'(Reynolds v. United States—1878). That is, Mormons are free to believe and say anything they like so long as they do not put their beliefs and words into actions of which the authorities disapprove. . . . You are free to express your religious views not because of their content but because of their status as expressions. Religious views in this understanding are just like other views—political views, aesthetic views, sexual views, baseball views—and what is valued about them is that they have been freely produced. . . . What is not valued about them is the content of what they urge" (*The Trouble with Principle*, [Cambridge: Harvard University Press, 1999], pp. 38–39).

56. Cited in Kraynak, *Christian Faith and Modern Democracy*, p. 24.

57. Fish, *Trouble with Principle*, p. 257.

58. J. S. McClelland, *A History of Western Political Thought* (London and New York: Routledge, 1996), 98. This is one place where H. R. Niebuhr is particularly troubling. In his chapter "Christ and Culture in Paradox," that is, the "dualism" chapter, he never raises the possibility that we are social beings. He organizes his whole project around individuals and theological concepts, never along the lines of belonging and allegiance. That would work if we really were "bubbles floating on a sea of nothingness."

59. Niebuhr is really quite evasive. In the grand finale of *Christ and Culture*, "Christ the Transformer of Culture," he says with great conviction that the kingdom of God is not "human progress in culture," but a divinely, universally transformed culture. Christian cultures or societies are an aberration—they undermine the universality of the kingdom. So, the kingdom of God will happen through humanity, universally, but this is not human progress. One gets the feeling that Niebuhr is a Rauschenbusch minus Schleiermacher's liberalism, and plus Tillich's crisis theology. Yet the outcome looks remarkably like the social gospel.

60. We are alluding here to Yoder's *The Priestly Kingdom: Social Ethics as Gospel* (Notre Dame, Ind.: University of Notre Dame Press, 1984). He criticizes Augustine for the doctrine of the true but invisible church. This doctrine, in Yoder's estimation, undermined the church's ability to practice the politics of Jesus because it had to deal with unbelievers as if they were believers. Christians could no longer assume the gathered community was the true church, "as a result, therefore, the eyes of those looking for the church had to turn to the clergy, especially to the episcopacy, and henceforth 'the church' meant the hierarchy more than the people" (p. 136). It is ironic that Augustine ends up rejected by both H. R. Niebuhr and Yoder. He is a failure, in the end, because even though he laid the groundwork for "Christ the Transformer of Culture,"

he compromised all of his insights because of his "defensiveness"(p. 216). His whole doctrine of two cities ends up being the worst kind of dualism, all, apparently, due to a lack of self-esteem. So, Augustine is rejected in the end by Niebuhr because he loses hope for the transformation of culture, and by Yoder because he loses hope for the purity of the church.

61. Augustine, *City of God,* book 11, chapter 1.

62. There are a number of strategies to maintain limits on power. Liberalism is such a strategy with its separation of church and state. But, as has been shown, that strategy actually gives ultimate power to the state and to commerce. John Courtney Murray's "mediating structures" are a neo-conservative attempt at separating the powers, and so is, but to a smaller degree, the Republicanism of the Founding Fathers, which is so admired by Robert Bellah. The trouble with all these strategies is that they are one-dimensional. A Christian view would argue for separation of powers on the grounds that our lives have an ultimate, heavenly dimension that can never fall under the authority of the state. This is not a private right, but a principle for subdividing memberships. It says the ultimate telos of life is not a democracy, but a kingdom. (See Kraynak, *Christian Faith and Modern Democracy,* p. 206.)

Richard Hooker gives us an early version of what has been called sphere sovereignty. He separates different portions of life under different kinds of laws (*Of the Laws of Ecclesiastical Polity* [Elicott City, Md.: Via Media, 1994], book 1, chapter 1:2). He, however, assumes a unified culture, including church and state, that is, Christendom, so he really does not entertain the thought of competing communal loyalties (the Anglican Church is for him "the Catholic Church in England"). Kuyper's sphere sovereignty gets more directly to the issue, because it does know a divided society. Kuyper does maintain a kind of Augustinian respect for creation. He probably, however, goes too far with the doctrine of common grace when he begins to talk about the *development* of culture (Abraham Kuyper, *Lectures on Calvinism* [Grand Rapids: Eerdmans, 1931], p. 30). He is still living under the assumption that there are only two interlocutors: Christians and Enlightenment liberals.

Kraynak is interesting because he argues that from a Christian view, prudentially, the optimal (if we can really call any earthly city optimal) government is monarchial constitutional democracy. The argument is complex and compelling, but it all happens under the heading of prudence, because the state is ordained by God for only very limited purposes.

Yoder (*Priestly Kingdom,* "The Christian Case for Democracy") is also interesting, because he argues for limits on power simply because Christians should not want it. That is "what the gentiles do." Christians should not think in terms of controlling society, even with limits, because that ultimately includes force. We should accept our diaspora situation as a minority community practicing a minority faith. We should, however, address society with the ethics of Jesus, not in terms of natural law, but in Jesus' own words. So, we should respect and listen to our neighbors not because of their innate rights or relationship to us in a fictional social contract. We should listen to and respect our neighbor, who may be a foreigner or even an enemy, because to be the church is to eschew power. "So democracy, when thus defined, does not simply mean that most people get to talk or that everybody gets counted. It means a theologically mandatory vesting of the right of dissent"(p. 168).

The problem with Yoder, and why we prefer Augustine, is that he does not recognize the "tares" in the church—even a church one joins freely (just think of Ananias and Sapphira); nor does he recognize our legitimate loyalties in "the earthly city."

63. Elshtain, *Augustine and the Limits of Politics*, p. 102 (citing Augustine, *City of God*, book 14, chapter 1).

64. Ibid., p. 103.

65. Ibid., pp. 101–5.

66. *City of God*, book 19, chapter 17.

Chapter 5

1. See "El plan espiritual de Aztlán" in *Aztlán: Essays on the Chicano Homeland*, ed. Rudolfo Anaya and Francisco Lomeli (Albuquerque: University of New Mexico Press, 1991), pp. 1–5.

2. See Rafael Perez-Torres, "Refiguring Aztlán," in *Postcolonial Theory and the United States: Race, Ethnicity and Literature* (Jackson: University of Mississippi Press), pp. 103–21. Perez-Torres describes how the Chicano poet Alurista, the original voice behind the "Plan espiritual de Aztlán" document, disappointed the militant faction at the conference by disavowing a separatist-nationalist program.

3. Rudolfo Anaya, "Aztlán, a Homeland without Borders," in *Aztlán: Essays on the Chicano Homeland*, ed. Rudolfo Anaya and Francisco Lomeli (Albuquerque: University of New Mexico Press, 1991), pp. 230–41.

4. Virgilio Elizondo, *Galilean Journey: The Mexican-American Promise* (Maryknoll, N.Y.: Orbis, 1983).

5. Even more regrettable, given our predominant focus on Latino writers, is our omission of important Puerto Rican voices (Edward Rivera, Judith Ortiz Cofer, and Esmeralda Santiago among them). Even though this group of authors is most accomplished, and relevant to the issues we are discussing, their work does not face the issues of borderlands and border-crossing in terms as obvious and intentional as does that of the authors we examine.

6. Margarite Fernández-Olmos, *Rudolfo A. Anaya: A Critical Companion* (Westport, Conn.: Greenwood, 1999), pp. 84–102.

7. Rudolfo Anaya, *Bless Me, Ultima* (Berkeley: Quinto Sol, 1972).

8. Kevin McIlvoy, "A Dialogue: Rudolfo Anaya/John Nichols," in *Conversations with Rudolfo Anaya*, ed. Bruce Dick and Silvio Sirias (Jackson: University of Mississippi Press, 1998), pp. 53–80.

9. Rudolfo Anaya, *Alburquerque* (Albuquerque: University of New Mexico Press, 1992), p. 106.

10. Marc Simmons, *Albuquerque: A Narrative History* (Albuquerque: University of New Mexico Press, 1982).

11. See Setha Low, *On the Plaza: The Politics of Public Space and Culture* (Austin: University of Texas Press, 2000), pp. 31–44.

12. Rodney Clapp, *A Peculiar People: The Church as Culture in a Post-Christian Society* (Downers Grove, Ill.: InterVarsity Press, 1996), p. 116.

13. Anaya, *Alburquerque*, p. 119.

14. For an understanding of political proceduralism, see Stephen Macedo, ed., *Deliberative Politics: Essays on Democracy and Disagreement* (New York: Oxford University Press, 1999).

15. Anaya, *Alburquerque*, p. 118.

16. For a thorough account of the now-global battle over water, see Jim Shulz's series of reports titled "Globalization and the War for Water in Bolivia," online at americas.org.

17. Anaya, *Alburquerque*, p. 239.

18. C. S. Lewis, *That Hideous Strength* (London: Bodley Head, 1945).

19. We are of the opinion that there is more to be gained from Lewis's imaginative work than from his rational apologetics. Our reference to his work in this particular comparative context underscores the enduring value of his fiction—for the issues with which it grapples.

20. Gloria Anzaldúa, *Borderlands/La Frontera: The New Mestiza* (San Francisco: Aunt Lute Press, 1987), pp. 2–3.

21. Ibid., p. 73.

22. This idea is present in the "woodwork" of Rodney Clapp's essay collection *Border Crossings: Christian Trespasses on Popular Culture and Public Affairs* (Grand Rapids: Brazos, 2000). We share the view that borders of all types are inevitable and inevitably trespassed.

23. Anzaldúa, *Borderlands/La Frontera*, p. 194.

24. Ibid., p. 31.

25. Ibid., p. 46.

26. A notable exception to this is Denis Lynn Heyck's anthology *Barrios and Borderlands: Cultures of Latinos and Latinas in the United States* (London: Routledge, 1994), which includes a selection by Elizondo and a brilliant line-up of Latino ecclesial voices.

27. Elizondo, *Galilean Journey*, p. 51.

28. Ibid., p. 52.

29. Anzaldúa, *Borderlands/La Frontera*, p. 19.

30. Elizondo, *Galilean Journey*, p. 58.

31. Ibid., p. 101.

32. Ibid., p. 122.

33. Ibid., p. 120.

34. Anzaldúa, *Borderlands/La Frontera*, p. 194.

35. Elizondo, *Galilean Journey*, p. 101.

36. Sandra Cisneros, *The House on Mango Street* (New York: Vintage Contemporaries, 1984).

37. Ibid., p. 97.

38. Ibid., p. 110.

39. Deborah Madsden, *Understanding Contemporary Chicana Literature* (Columbia: University of South Carolina Press, 2000), pp. 105–34.

40. Cisneros, *My Wicked, Wicked Ways* (New York: Vintage, 1991).

41. Ilan Stavans, "Sandra Cisneros: Form over Content," in the *Essential Ilan Stavans* (New York: Routledge, 2000), pp. 41–46.

42. This is part of the jacket-cover endorsement. Terkel's praise is joined to that of Latin American authors Elena Poniatowska and Eduardo Galeano.

43. Cisneros, *Caramelo* (New York: Knopf, 2002), pp. 389–90.

44. Ibid., p. 390.

45. Ibid., pp. 424–25.

46. Foreword (Sandra Cisneros) to Virgilio Elizondo's *The Future Is Mestizo: Life Where Cultures Meet* (Boulder: University Press of Colorado, 2000), pp. ix–xi.

47. Cisneros, *Caramelo*, pp. 17–18.

Chapter 6

1. Cited in Robert P. Kraynak, *Christian Faith and Modern Democracy: God and Politics in the Fallen World,* (Notre Dame, Ind.: University of Notre Dame Press, 2001), p. 141.

2. Alasdair MacIntyre (*After Virtue: A Study In Moral Theory,* [Notre Dame, Ind.: University of Notre Dame Press, 1984], p. 12) calls this view *emotivism*. Emotivism is the doctrine that all evaluative judgments and, more specifically, all moral judgments are nothing but expressions of preference, expressions of attitude or feeling, insofar as they are moral or evaluative in character.

3. Francis Martin, *The Feminist Question: Feminist Theology in the Light of Christian Tradition* (Grand Rapids: Eerdmans, 1994), p. 185.

4. As it turns out, when separated from theology, the very idea of "rights" is an assertion based on nothing at all—no tradition or community or authority. Kraynak (*Christian Faith and Modern Democracy*, pp. 30–31) lists "two fundamental movements of the liberal paradigm: (1) skepticism or doubt about knowing the greatest good when it is handed down as higher wisdom; and (2) confidence in the individuals and nations to determine their fate by thinking on their own. . . . But the same formula also contains the fatal flaw of liberalism, for the skepticism or doubt which brings emancipation from traditional authority and the recognition of universal human dignity eventually leaves that dignity with no grounding at all in reality and with few resources to resist the pressures of modern mass society."

MacIntyre (*After Virtue*, pp. 68–69) spells out just how "rights" lacks any grounding in reality: "The best reason for asserting so bluntly that there are no such rights is indeed precisely the same type as the best reason which we possess for asserting that there are no witches and the best reason which we possess for asserting that there are no unicorns: every attempt to give good reasons for believing that there *are* such rights has failed. The eighteenth-century philosophical defenders of natural rights sometimes suggest that the assertions which state that men possess them are self-evident truths; but we know that there are no self-evident truths. Twentieth-century moral philosophers have sometimes appealed to their and our intuitions; but one of the things that we ought to have learned from the history of moral philosophy is that the introduction of the word 'intuition' by a moral philosopher is always a signal that something has gone badly wrong with an argument."

5. By any account, reading all forms of ordination rites in the catholic tradition, looking at the pertinent passages of Scripture, as well as the tradition of apostolic succession, the authority of an *episcopas* or of a presbyter is a *charism,* that is, it does not reside in an individual, but in a person in the church, who has a definite task of guarding doctrine and must be morally exemplary. This one person is to be a model for the whole community. So, Zizioulas writes, "The bishop in his function is the apostles' successor inasmuch as he is the image of Christ within the community" (*Being and Communion,* p. 116) (once again, we see in the bishop the general *"as-so"* [Volf] or conformation to the image of Christ [Radner] pattern, which applies to all the people of God).

6. Thomas Jefferson, Letter to Peter Corr, 10 August 1787, in *The Life and Selected Writings of Thomas Jefferson,* ed. Adrienne Koch and William Peden (New York: Random/Modern Library, 1944), pp. 431–33.

7. Kraynak, *Christian Faith and Modern Democracy,* p. 148.

8. Ibid., p. 152.

9. *Social Gospel* as cited in ibid., pp. 142–43.

10. Kraynak looks at the story as received, and debunks it, showing at length that the Christian tradition has been quite illiberal and undemocratic; see chapter 2 of *Christian Faith and Modern Democracy,* "The Illiberal and Undemocratic Christian Tradition," pp. 45–106.

11. Rodney Clapp, *Peculiar People*, p. 25.

12. Kraynak provides us with a trenchant account of how the City of God slowly changed into the City of Man in America. "To understand how America arrived at this republican religion, one may read with great profit an article by the historian Paul Johnson titled, 'God and the Americans.' Johnson's thesis is that America has always been a religious nation—'a nation with the soul of a church,' in the words of Chesterton. But the American religion is hard to define because it evolved gradually from the Puritanism of the colonial era to the Deism of the founding period, producing a republican civil religion that mixed elements of Evangelical Protestantism and Enlightenment liberalism—a combination of Calvin and Locke, as it were. It survives today in what is

loosely called the Judeo-Christian tradition which Americans appeal to when they recite the Pledge of Allegiance to the Flag and pay tribute to the republic as 'one nation under God.' This is the journey from Cotton Mather's Magnalia Christi Americana to the later mission, articulated fully by Woodrow Wilson's 'Fourteen Points,' of spreading democratic human rights around the world" (*Christian Faith and Modern Democracy,* pp. 128–29). Also, H. Richard Niebuhr, in *The Kingdom of God in America* (Middletown, Conn.: Wesleyan University Press, 1988; rpt. of 1937 ed., New York: Harper and Row), explains at length the journey from Puritanism to Social Gospel liberalism. His conclusions are somewhat ironic, namely, that the kingdom of God always creates a crisis for the kingdoms of this world. This thesis can be harmonized with Christ transforming culture if the church exists to change the culture, but the church should never think of itself as its own peculiar culture. When it does, in his opinion, it loses its very purpose for existence (see *Christ and Culture,* [New York: Harper and Row, 1951), pp. 217–18.)

13. Stanley Hauerwas, *With the Grain of the Universe: The Church's Witness and Natural Theology* (Grand Rapids: Brazos, 2001), p. 83.

14. Kallistos Ware, *The Orthodox Way,* rev. ed. (Crestwood, N.Y.: St. Vladimir's Seminary Press, 2001), p. 53.

15. Karl Barth, *Church Dogmatics* 4/1, p. 41.

16. This insight is drawn from Roger Lundin, *Culture of Interpretation: Christian Faith and the Postmodern World,* (Grand Rapids: Eerdmans, 1993), pp. 128–29. "In the spirit of contemporary theory, the conception of thought as an expression of gratitude—in anything but a self-congratulatory form—seems unfathomable. Emerson's 'Self-Reliance' defines as well as anything the nature of gratitude in modernity: 'In every work of genius we recognize our own rejected thoughts: they come back to us with a certain alienated majesty.' For several hundred years in Western intellectual life, the form of gratitude that has seemed superior to all others is that of the self thanking itself for whatever freedom it has attained or whatever satisfaction it has acquired."

17. Stanley Hauerwas and Charles Pinches, *Christians among the Virtues: Theological Conversations with Ancient and Modern Ethics* (Notre Dame, Ind.: University of Notre Dame Press, 1997); see chapter 8, "Is Obedience a Virtue?"

18. Ibid., p. 138.

19. Ibid., pp. 134–35.

20. Stanley Fish, in *The Trouble with Principle,* works with Milton and Augustine on this topic. He writes, "The difference between a believer and a non-believer is not that one reasons and the other doesn't but that one reasons from a first premise the other denies; and from this difference flow others that make the fact that both are reasoning a sign not of commonality but of its absence" (p. 263). Commenting on *On Christian Doctrine,* "Since you know that in a world ordered by a just and benevolent God everything signifies his love for us and our obligation to love our fellow creatures for his sake, struggle with what the world presents to you until you are able to discern

that signification" (p. 265). In *Paradise Lost,* "Satan is the very type of those who would reason before they believe. . . . Purge the soul first by orienting it to the appropriate object of desire, and then reason, for only then, says Augustine, are you 'capable of receiving reason,' capable, that is of engaging in reasoning that is not endlessly spinning its own wheels" (p. 267).

21. After the bread is broken in the celebration, the priest says, "Alleluia, Christ our Passover is sacrificed for us" and the people reply "Therefore let us keep the feast, Alleluia" or in Spanish, *Celebramos la fiesta!*

22. We are dependent on Roger Lundin in this whole section on Communion in early America and Emerson's place in that story, especially on chapter 5, "Emerson and the Spirit of Theory," of *Culture of Interpretation.*

23. *Emerson in His Journals,* 71, cited by Lundin, *Culture of Interpretation,* pp. 113–14.

24. Lundin, *Culture of Interpretation,* pp. 124–25.

25. *Emerson in His Journals,* pp. 77, 80, cited by Lundin, *Culture of Interpretation,* p. 114.

26. Lundin, *Culture of Interpretation,* p. 263.

27. Kraynak writes in *Christian Faith and Modern Democracy,* "The professed neutrality of the liberal state about the Good Life is merely a pretext for imposing an exclusive view of the Good life. Though claiming to take no stand on the ultimate purpose for life, modern liberal democracy in fact promotes a life dedicated to middle-class materialism, popular entertainment, and secular humanism which it imposes through the aggressive marketing of modern culture in public education, the universities, the courts, mass media, and other instruments of opinion formation that many critics of mass society have aptly described as social tyranny. . . . Stated succinctly, modern liberal democracy proclaims in principle but subverts in practice the dignity of man" (*Christian Faith and Modern Democracy,* pp. 201–202).

28. Hans Georg Gadamer, *Truth and Method,* rev. ed. (New York: Continuum, 1989), p. 12.

29. We summarize Anaya, using occasional quotations from pp. 105–17.

30. John Rosemond, *Six-Point Plan for Raising Happy, Healthy Children* (Kansas City, Mo.: Andrews and McMeel, 1989), 7. The rest of the quote powerfully furthers the point: "Well, if you want raising children to be difficult, you need only put them first in your family, and it will be. By putting your children first in your family, you guarantee they will become manipulative, demanding, and unappreciative of anything and everything you do for them. You guarantee they will grow up believing they can do as they please, that it's unfair for you to expect them to lift a finger of responsibility around the home, and that it's your bounden duty to give them everything they want and serve them in every conceivable way. Putting children first in the family further guarantees that you will experience parenthood as one of the most frustrating and unrewarding things you've ever done. It further guarantees the ultimate unhappiness of your children, because happiness is achieved only by

accepting responsibility for one's self, not by being led to believe that someone else is responsible for you"(p. 7).

31. Rodney Clapp provides a thorough account of the family in the Bible in *Family at the Crossroads: Beyond Traditional and Modern Options* (Downers Grove, Ill.: InterVarsity Press, 1993).

32. Barbara Dafoe Whitehead (*The Divorce Culture* [New York: Random House, 1998]) writes, "The traditional definition of "family" as formed through marriage, blood, and adoption gave way to a new definition that emphasized the quality and content of affectionate bonds over bonds of blood or marriage" (132). "As social fact it is the institutional mechanism linking a man and woman to their biological children. Marriage establishes the social and geographic identity of the family; it is through marriage that a child claims support and affection from one identified father and one mother living together in a common household. Marriage also establishes the economic bases of the family; it provides the institutional mechanism for transferring resources from the older to the younger generation, for recruiting help from relatives, and especially for attaching fathers to their biological children and securing sustained and regular paternal investment in their offspring" (p. 137). She then gives us a catalog of problems with the modern family that is based on voluntary affections. "First, it is vulnerable to disruption and thus inherently unstable. Affections waver, fade, or die, and ties based on affections can weaken or dissolve. . . . At the same time that affectionate marriage fosters high parental investments in the couple's children, it also provides a shaky institutional foundation for childrearing. . . . In this system of family relationships there is an underlying tension between the contingency of marital bonds and the permanence of parent-child bonds. The very idea that voluntary ties of affection can serve as a reliable basis for permanent attachments and binding obligation seems foolhardy" (pp. 138–39).

33. See Clapp, *Families at the Crossroads,* pp. 69–73.

34. See Wayne Dosick, *Living Judaism: The Complete Guide to Jewish Belief, Tradition, and Practice* (New York: HarperSanFrancisco, 1995), pp. 293–95.

35. Clapp, *Families at the Crossroads,* pp. 67–68.

36. Augustine, *City of God,* book 19, ch. 19.

37. Our thoughts on the handing on of tradition are adapted from Michael Goldberg, "Discipleship: Basing One Life on Another—It's Not What you Know, It's Who You Know," in *Theology without Foundations: Religious Practice and the Future of Theological Truth,* ed. Stanley Hauerwas, Nancy Murphy, Mark Nation (Nashville: Abingdon, 1994).

38. Cited in ibid., p. 291.

39. Understood in these terms, when bishops or presbyters act outside of the tradition or the community, they renounce their ordination. Individuals cannot invent doctrine, and ecclesial authority is just that—it is a *charism* in a person in a community—neither an ontological change in an individual

granting them some supernatural power and access to God, nor merely a function in a club. (See Zizioulas, *Being as Communion,* ch. 6, "Ministry and Communion.")

Epilogue

1. Augustine, *Confessions,* book 1, chapter 1.